VALLEY WALLS

VALLEY WALLS

A Memoir of Climbing & Living in Yosemite

GLEN DENNY

YOSEMITE CONSERVANCY
Yosemite National Park

(opposite) Dihedral Wall, El Capitan

Yosemite Conservancy wishes to thank the family of Donald Prevett for the generous donation that helped make this book possible.

Text copyright © 2016 by Glen Denny

All photographs except those appearing on pages 18, 32, 62, 168, and 172 copyright © by Glen Denny

Yosemite Valley map © 2016 by Eric Knight, inspired by H.C. Berann.

Additional credits:

18: "Cliffs of Royal Arches, Half Dome, Yosemite National Park, California," circa 1950. Photograph by Ansel Adams. Copyright © 2016.

32: "Mount Whitney in Black and White," copyright © by Eric Tressler, reprinted by permission of Eric Tressler/eric-tressler.artistwebsites.com.

62: Photograph copyright © by Evan Russel, reprinted by permission of Evan Russel.

143–44: Adapted from "Quicksilver," published in *Alpinist* 17, Autumn 2006.

161: William Wordsworth, "Lines Written a Few Miles above Tintern Abbey," 1798.

161: Jack Kerouac, *The Dharma Bums.* (New York: The Viking Press, 1958), 58.

168: Photograph copyright © Keith Walklet, reprinted by permission of Keith Walklet.

172: Half Dome. Ralph Anderson, Yosemite Museum, Archives, and Research Library, National Park Service, RL 636.

175: Let's Do It (Let's Fall in Love) (from *Paris*). Words and Music by Cole Porter. Copyright © 1928 (Renewed) WB Music Corp. All Rights Reserved. Used By Permission of Alfred Music.

YOSEMITE
CONSERVANCY.

FSC
www.fsc.org
MIX
Paper from
responsible sources
FSC® C103061

yosemiteconservancy.org

Library of Congress Control Number: 2015956065

Cover and text design by Nancy Austin
ISBN 978-1-930238-63-3
Printed on recycled paper made from sustainable sources.
Printed in the USA by Jostens, Inc., represented by Qualibre, Inc.

1 2 3 4 5 6 — 20 19 18 17 16

To my wife,
Marguerite sans Peur

Mount Conness
Southwest Face

Mount Whitney
East Face

Half Dome
Southwest Face
The Diving Board

Lost Lake

Royal Arches
Arches Route

Yosemite Falls
Yosemite Point Buttress
The Lost Arrow
Sunnyside Bench

Washington Column
East Face

Glacier Point
The Apron

THE AHWAHNEE

CAMP CURRY

YOSEMITE VILLAGE

Staircase Falls

Sentinel Rock

OLD VILLAGE

Lower Brother
Michael's Ledge

YOSEMITE LODGE

CAMP 4

Manure Pile Buttress
After Six

El Capitan
Dihedral Wall
The Nose
North America Wall

Leaning Tower
West Face

Lower Cathedral Rock
North Buttress

YOSEMITE VALLEY

The Rostrum
North Face

Contents

(opposite) Yosemite Valley, showing most of the routes included in this book

Gary Colliver in Camp 4

Foreword

Glen Denny and I met when we took part in the first ascent of the most noteworthy Yosemite climb of 1959, the East Face of the Washington Column. This fearsome wall was the brainchild of Warren Harding, well known for his iconic first ascent of El Capitan a year earlier. Although neither Glen nor I led a single pitch (we mainly acted as a support group, carrying water and supplies to Warren and his partner, Chuck Pratt) we were pleased to be on a big wall at last. There would be many more, as Glen so eloquently writes in this book.

But our Column adventure—and others of that era—illustrates the remarkable changes in all aspects of rock climbing that have taken place over half a century, not only in Yosemite but worldwide. In the 1950s and 1960s we hammered pitons by the thousands into cracks that turned out to be more easily damaged than we could then imagine. We used 120-foot braided ropes that snarled into unforgiving tangles. On big climbs we placed fixed ropes that stretched from the bottom of a cliff to near the top. We slept without pads on small ledges or even stood all night in slings, lashed to a few pitons and praying for dawn. We took our time, proud that we were as safe as our mentors had taught us to be. When ascending our fixed lines we used cumbersome prusik knots attached to the rope and, using foot slings, laboriously struggled upward, taking half an hour to advance a hundred and twenty feet.

Now jump ahead fifty years, gradually, to be sure. Overuse of pitons had scarred the cracks on many a route, and so all sorts of clever devices not requiring a hammer appeared—and the granite was spared. Rope length shot up to nearly two hundred feet or, in the modern parlance, sixty meters—and these colorful perlon lines were as smooth as silk. Fixing ropes up cliffs soon ceased, and new first ascents thus became even more challenging. Portable ledges with shelters appeared, ensuring a good night's rest (sleep lulled by radio music and, later, by every new device the computer age could turn out). Speed climbing and solo climbing became increasingly popular, and a route such as our Washington Column climb, renamed Astroman following its free ascent, was sometimes climbed rope-less in a few hours. Harding and Pratt, among the best climbers of their day, had used direct aid most of the way! Prusik knots, thank God, were no longer to be seen; mechanical clamps made ascents far easier.

Just as Glen and I once devoured books about the really old days (amazed that anyone could get up intimidating cliffs using crude handmade pitons or, on snow, progress upward using alpenstocks and Tricouni nails on their outlandish boots), modern climbers benefit from the experiences from our active careers—if only to wonder how the hell we did it using such primitive gear.

Climbers of the 1950s and '60s mostly weren't star athletes. In the off-season we rarely worked out and had to get into shape by climbing easy stuff early in the spring. Glen was an exception. Tall and thin, he had no bulging biceps or rock-hard forearms. But did the man have endur-ance! His runs up Half Dome and his incredible circuits of the High Sierra Camps astonished us all, though we also wondered if he wasn't just a little crazy to punish his body so hideously. This endurance, of course, helped his rock climbing, and his later trips to icy South American peaks suited him just fine.

In the early 1960s, Camp 4, the climbers' hangout then and now, was an expansive place, more or less divided into two sections. The lower one in summer was occupied mostly by tourists whom we gently mocked for their trailers and sites swept clean of those horrid pine needles. The upper sloping section was more chaotic, with no official sites, and tour-ists shunned this area. Fine with us! We put down our tents anywhere we liked. In the off-season, in the early 1960s, Camp 4 was deserted during weekdays, with perhaps ten climbers up the slope and the same number of tourists down in their manicured area.

We climbers were a bit rebellious and uncouth, and occasional uneasy encounters with park rangers became inevitable as they enforced campground stay limits. Our presence at the nearby Yosemite Lodge on non-climbing days annoyed janitors, waitresses, and the suits, but it was a public place, of course. Glen and I were virtually alone in the Lodge's lounge, reading in front of a huge fire, listening to the rain pattering down outside, when we heard of President Kennedy's assassination.

This time of solitude didn't last. America was changing, with better highways, more leisure time, more disposable income. My 1964 guidebook to the Valley, the first one ever, brought an influx of climbers almost immediately. In the ensuing decades, with countless newer guides, Camp 4 became a crowded township with hundreds of big-wall seekers camped a few yards apart from each other. Tourists need not apply.

Throughout Glen's journeys his camera was never out of arm's reach. His lens rarely interfered with our daily camp activities, and on the walls his leader or belayer never knew when they would become the stars of many of his later published photographs. These photos, and now his stories, brilliantly capture the essence of that time.

Steve Roper
Oakland, California
March 2016

Author's Note

This is a book of stories about climbing and living in Yosemite from 1958 to 1965. Although all the people and events described are real, this work is neither a documentary history nor a comprehensive autobiography. Rather, it is an evocation of Valley life as experienced by the denizens of Camp 4 during what has since been named the Golden Age of Yosemite climbing.

This memoir is based on my notes and photographs and, especially, my vivid recollections of those times, which play in my mind like a film. In a few instances, events and scenes have been combined for narrative economy.

Acknowledgments

I would like to thank the following for contributing their expertise and memories in the writing of this book: Allen Berrey, Gary Colliver, Frank Gronberg, John Rawlings, Steve Roper, and Greg Stock.

In addition, many thanks to the staff of the Yosemite Conservancy as well as to the editors, designers, and proofreaders who participated in this book's development and production: Nancy Austin, Peggy Denny, Joanne Farness, Nicole Geiger, Chris Jones, Eric Knight, and DeAnne Musolf, and to Evan Russel of The Ansel Adams Gallery.

Yosemite Valley

PROLOGUE
Into the Valley

Beneath my feet I could see the river, winding through the meadows two thousand feet below. It was spring, and I was sitting on the summit of the Lower Brother in Yosemite Valley. Waterfalls leaped from the Valley rim, surging down in columns of white froth. The river was full and smooth. The meadows were lush and green.

The Lower Brother projected out into the Valley, and I was surrounded by sheer rock on all sides. It looked like a sculpture garden of all possible granite forms: walls and buttresses, spires and domes, aprons and arches.

The path that led me here began with trout. When I was in grammar school, my father took me on fishing trips in the Sierra Nevada. The highlight of each summer was a backpacking trip into the Evolution country, after golden trout. In high school I became interested in bigger physical challenges and started scrambling up the peaks that rose above the lakes and streams we were fishing in.

I went on Explorer Scout treks, a week of trail rambling near timberline, where one of the objectives would be climbing the highest peak in the area. This plan worked well until we went to Humphreys Basin.

As soon as we saw Mount Humphreys, we realized that it was a very different kind of thing from the mountains we had been scrambling up. The side of the mountain facing us looked like a sheer wall. We knew nothing about real climbing and didn't realize a rope was required on even its easiest route. Our adult leaders took a closer look and declared it impossible—at least for us. The mountain was put off limits, and we scrambled up an easier peak.

But for some reason I kept looking at Humphreys. The idea of reaching its high, remote summit fascinated me. One evening I was looking at it through binoculars and noticed a long, thin shadow on its face. That shadow might be cast by a gully, I thought. Perhaps it could be climbed.

The next morning I told our leader that I wanted to hike up to Piute

Pass because I hadn't been to the crest of the Sierra on foot before. This was true enough. I didn't tell him what I really wanted to do because permission would have been denied. I hiked up to the pass with Dave Green, my best friend on the trip. After taking a break, we headed for Mount Humphreys.

As we got closer, it still didn't look climbable. A long talus gully went up left of the steep face and ended at a notch on the crest, left of the summit. From the notch we would be able to see the other side of the mountain, which might be easier. But when we got there our hopes were dashed. The other side was worse than what we had been looking at.

The game was up, but at least we had given it a good try. Then I remembered the gully I thought I had spotted with the binoculars. I hadn't seen it on the way up. We descended to the bottom of the sheer cliff. Dave had had enough and agreed to wait there while I took a look.

The gully, if it existed, had to be to the right. I traversed under the cliff, across talus chutes and ribs of solid rock, until I reached a steep, narrow gully that shot up the wall toward the summit. This must be it! The rock was smoother than anything I had climbed before, but I managed to get up it by squeezing into cracks. The next problem was a big boulder wedged in the gully. I couldn't figure out how to climb it but discovered a chimney to the left that let me bypass the chockstone. After traversing back into the gully above the boulder, I stuffed my bandanna into a crack to mark the place for my return. I felt very good about solving that problem and charged up the gully to the crest, just right of the summit.

Now I was close to my goal and feeling quite excited. But I could go no farther. The next problem was a smooth wall I couldn't climb in my loose, worn-out hiking boots. Fortunately, I had enough sense to back off before I broke my neck.[1]

Although I didn't reach the summit, it was an exhilarating experience. I'd never been so high in the air before. When I looked down the other side of the mountain, Owens Valley seemed impossibly far below. A hundred new mountains had come into view, and I could see sixty lakes.

At the same time, it was very frustrating. Other people had reached the summit, why couldn't I? Instinctively, I felt that learning how to solve problems like this would provide great satisfaction.

My first year of college began that fall. I spent a lot of time in the library, but all I wanted to read were climbing books. I was hooked. The next fall, for the first time since kindergarten, I didn't go back to school. I had heard that there was a lot of climbing in Yosemite. And there was a year-round tourist industry, so you could get a job, live there, and climb—all at the same time. It seemed like the perfect solution.

Back at home, I packed up my car and waved good-bye. As I drove down the street, I could see my parents in the rear-view mirror, waving back. I knew they were disappointed. Why was I wasting my education and throwing myself into such a useless activity? At times, during the long winter, I had wondered, too. But now, looking at the Valley from my eyrie, I knew I had made the right decision.

I had reached the summit of Lower Brother by climbing Michael's Ledge, a route that was rated class 4.[2] That meant you should be belayed on a rope by a partner, in case of a fall. I didn't have a rope or a partner, but I wanted to see what it was like.

At first the ledge was broad and easy. But as it diagonaled up the wall, it narrowed down to a thin staircase, with some of the steps missing. The rock was solid and I searched it carefully for the best sequence of hand- and footholds. I had been over some exposure on Mount Humphreys, but it wasn't anything like this. For the first time, a drop of a thousand feet was straight below my heels. I tried not to look at the road between my feet and the little cars creeping along it. There was no reason to fall, I kept telling myself. Just stay calm. If I could keep my emotions under control, all would be well.

Farther on, I came to a place that was less exposed but harder to climb. After ascending it, I immediately climbed back down while the moves were still fresh in my mind, and climbed back up again. This calmed my fears about the descent, and I continued on with growing confidence.

On the summit I looked down at the smooth walls that led up to my perch. That's where the real climbs were: the West Face and the Southwest Arête. The route I had done was only the descent route for the serious climbs.

Across the Valley I could see the north face of Sentinel Rock. I knew that sheer wall had been climbed. Up the Valley I could see the Lost Arrow, the spire that became John Salathé's lodestone. Beyond that was Half Dome. Its great face had been climbed once, two years earlier.

I wanted to climb them, but they were far beyond my skills. I was looking at walls climbed by John Salathé, but the rocks I had been climbing were no more difficult than those ascended by Edward Whymper in the Alps long ago. I was a century behind!

It had been September 1958 when I left school and home and drove to Yosemite Valley. When I reached El Capitan Meadow I ran into a traffic jam.[3] I assumed it was a "bear jam" typical of national parks at the time. The bears had learned to sit up in cute poses on the side of the road, begging for food, and this was irresistible to the tourists. They stopped their cars—thus stopping all traffic—got out, and tossed doughnuts and marshmallows to the bears. They took photos and movies, and sometimes they tried to get into the picture with the bear—not a good idea.

There was nothing to do but get out of the car and look around, but I didn't see any bears. Instead, everyone was looking up at El Capitan, pointing up and talking excitedly about climbers. I borrowed some binoculars and scanned the wall.

El Capitan looked quite vertical and blank. I could see why it had never been climbed. A few cracks wandered up here and there, but they started and stopped in the middle of nowhere, surrounded by immense plaques of flawless granite.

I kept moving the glasses and suddenly I encountered a tiny human figure, halfway up the wall. He was moving up very slowly, with a kind of swimming motion. I couldn't see what kept him from falling. A hundred feet lower I saw another man, sitting on a ledge, looking up at him. The tourists said they had been up there for days, living on that wall.

It was the most inspiring thing I had ever seen. Instantly I realized I had come to the right place. I didn't know how they were doing it, but I was going to find out.

Warren Harding on the Leaning Tower

1
Learning to Climb

My first job in Yosemite was bussing dishes in the Yosemite Lodge cafeteria. My roommate, Rob McKnight, ran the dishwashing machine. He was from Chicago, and after a year of college he had come out west in search of adventure. I convinced him that climbing might be the answer to his quest.

I had mail-ordered some gear from the Ski Hut in Berkeley: rope, boots, ice ax, carabiners, and fifty feet of one-inch nylon webbing for making runners and rappel anchors. I didn't order any pitons because that seemed too advanced. First we would learn the basics before going on to more complicated techniques.

On days off we would take the gear and walk up to the rocks with a guidebook in one hand and a how-to book in the other, and try to figure out how this kind of thing was done. By now I was used to class 3 climbing, where you didn't need a rope, but if you fell you might die. Next was class 4, where you used a rope because, without it, if you fell you would surely die, but the rope would save you if you used it correctly. So we studied the how-to book very carefully and learned how to belay and rappel.

It was the spring of 1959, and we started with climbs the guidebook called class 4: Sunnyside Bench, Lunch Ledge, and the Gunsight. These climbs got us to some exciting places but gave us only a small taste of the real thing.

I went over to Camp 4 because I'd heard that was where climbers stayed, and one day I met Warren Harding. He was easy to recognize from the photos that had been in the newspapers about the El Capitan ascent the previous November.

He was short, wiry, and intense, with long, black, swept-back hair that made him look more like a motorcycle gang member than a climber. But he laughed easily and liked to make jokes. He referred to Gaston Rébuffat, the French climber, as Ghastly Rubberfat. And he had put a bumper sticker on his car. Someone named Bonelli was running for sheriff in Sacramento, his hometown. Warren had altered the spelling so that it read "Bonatti for Sheriff," after the famous Italian climber Walter Bonatti.

I told him about the climbs Rob and I had been doing, and how we wanted to do bigger things.

"Well, come on, then," he said with a grin. "Let's go do some *real* climbing."

This was a breakthrough—now I could learn from an expert. I told Rob about it.

"Are you sure that was him?" he asked. "Why would he want to climb with beginners like us?"

"I don't know, but we've got to do it. This is our big chance."

On our next day off we got in Warren's car and drove down the Valley, past Rixon's Pinnacle and the Three Brothers. Before reaching El Capitan, he turned right onto a narrow dirt road that had no sign. After two hundred yards I could see a small, windowless cement building on the left. Painted on the door, in big red letters, were the words: DANGER! EXPLOSIVES!

"That's where they keep the dynamite for trail building, clearing rock-slides—stuff like that," Warren said. "And over there, on the right, is the biggest pile of horse manure you'll ever see. It's from the stables. I hear the gardeners use it for plantings around the buildings."

By now the road was just a pair of tire tracks. After another hundred yards it ended at a rock wall.

"So here it is," Warren said.

We got out and looked up at a steep wall several hundred feet high. "It doesn't really have a name. Sometimes I call it Powder House Buttress or Dynamite Buttress, but it's not impressive enough for that. So I guess it should be Manure Pile Buttress. Anyway, it's a good place to practice. The main route goes up that corner."

He pointed at a right-facing open book that shot up the wall. It looked much more serious than the things Rob and I had been climbing.

Warren opened the trunk of his car. Inside was a tangled heap of climbing gear: ropes, slings, hammers, and racks of pitons mixed up with ice axes, crampons, and even tent poles and a car jack. "I've got to get organized someday," he said as he grabbed a double armful and tossed it on the ground. He pawed through the pile, glancing up at the corner a couple of times, and picked out a dozen pitons of various sizes.

"That should do it," he said, clipping them onto a sling over his shoulder. He pulled out two ropes and some other gear, and we walked over to a tree close to the wall. It would be the belay anchor.

Warren uncoiled a rope and said, "OK. Lesson number one: How to tie in."

I thought we already knew how to do this but figured it wouldn't hurt to hear it from a real expert. We might learn some new tricks.

Warren put one end of the rope around his waist. He made a small loop with one hand—the beginning of a bowline knot—and brought the end of the rope up to it with his other hand. Then he started reciting the story that helps you remember how to tie it.

"So," he said, putting the rope end through the loop, "the squirrel comes out of the hole in the tree, runs around the trunk, and . . . no, that's not right. You know, every time I look at one of those how-to books I get totally confused." He paused, scratching his head.

"Oh, now I've got it. The rabbit comes out of his hole at the base of the tree, runs around the trunk, and then . . . and then . . . what does he do? I can't remember where he goes next."

Eventually he got it figured out. He anchored me to the tree, explained how to hip belay, and walked over to the rock.

"Now, before you start up, you always recheck everything. Bowline, shoelaces, pitons and carabiners on this side, runners on that side, hammer . . . oops, forgot my hammer." He walked rapidly back to the car. I couldn't pay out the rope fast enough, and he pulled on it, nearly knocking me over. The rope was getting caught on some rocks and bushes. Warren got to the car and started banging around in the trunk, shouting, "Where is that damn thing?"

While he was doing this, Rob came over to me and whispered in my ear: "Are you sure this is the right guy?"

I found out later that this was one of Harding's comedy routines. Anything that people took extremely seriously, he had to turn into a joke.

Warren returned to the wall and looked up. A small tree was growing horizontally out from the corner, about forty feet up. "I'll belay at that tree.

This rope isn't long enough to reach the top of the corner in one pitch."

He climbed up the smooth face, just right of the corner. I couldn't see the holds he was using, but he made it look as easy as climbing a ladder. After twenty feet he stopped and hammered in a piton, clipped the rope into it with a carabiner, and then continued up, jamming his left hand and foot into the corner crack and using invisible holds on the wall for his right hand and foot. He reached the tree and sat on its trunk, with his feet braced against the wall. After tying in and pulling up the extra rope until it was tight on my waist, he looked down between his legs and said, "OK. Come on."

This wasn't what I expected to hear. Rob and I had been studying the how-to book. In situations like this, the belayer and follower were supposed to exchange a precise sequence of commands.

Belayer: "On belay."

Follower: "Ready to climb."

Belayer: "Climb."

Follower: "Climbing."

I had mentioned this to Warren earlier, back in Camp 4. "Oh, really?" he chuckled. "I always wondered how they did that. Sounds like being in the army. I usually say something like: 'OK, Cliff King. Haul ass!'"

Rob pulled a second hammer out of the heap. I stuck it head down in the back pocket of my Levis, looped the sling over my shoulders, and started up my first pitch of class 5 rock.

Up close, there were more holds than I had expected: little edges for fingertips, wider places in the crack for my left foot, shallow dished-out pockets for my right foot. The problem was using them in the right sequence so I wouldn't fall off. I figured it out and arrived at the piton. After hammering it out, I looked up. The next section looked harder, with fewer holds. I moved up, trying to use the jam crack like Warren had, and searching for holds on the face. Warren started making suggestions, pointing out tiny holds between the big ones and saying, "Just put your toe in the crack and twist it. It'll stick."

My new Italian mountaineering boots weren't right for Yosemite. The toe was too thick to fit in the crack. Warren's rock shoes were thinner, more flexible, and fit his feet like gloves. The soles were cut flush with the uppers. On my boots the soles stuck out a quarter of an inch, leaving a flexible rim that rolled off small holds. But I made some long reaches past the hardest places and soon was sitting on the tree trunk next to Warren.

"How was that?" he asked.

"Great."

"Yeah, you did fine."

He was looking up the wall.

"Liked it, huh?"

"Sure. You bet."

"How'd you like to lead the next pitch?"

I took a quick glance to see if he was kidding. For once he seemed to be quite serious.

The route above the tree looked more difficult than what we'd done below. I pretended to look it over carefully, while trying to think of what to say. I wanted to do it, but I'd never even followed anything that hard, much less led it. This was too soon. I had never placed a piton before, but I didn't tell Warren because this seemed like my big chance.

"OK," I said.

He handed me the sling of hardware and some runners and put me on belay. I stood on the tree trunk and looked up. The rock here was steeper and smoother, but the crack in the corner ran all the way up, so at least I could place pitons for protection.

I stepped up onto the rock. The left wall bulged out, and I couldn't get my foot into the crack. The face on the right had no holds to stand on.

"Try cross-pressure," Warren suggested. "See the vertical edge of that little flake out on the right? Put your foot against it and push, like you were in a chimney."

This wasn't anything like a chimney, but there was nothing else to do, so I put my right foot out against the tiny flake and pushed, pressing the left side of my body against the bulge. By alternately wriggling my shoulder and hip up, I managed to gain a few inches.

"That's good," Warren said. "Do it again."

I found a little hold for my left foot in the crack, shifted my right foot to a higher flake, and moved up again.

"That's it. Keep going," Warren said.

I repeated the move, got past the bulge, and came to a ledge big enough for half of each foot.

"Great," Warren said. "That was the hardest part of the climb. Now, put in some protection."

I picked out the widest piton, a one-and-a-half-inch angle and inserted it halfway into the crack by hand. The how-to book said that was just right. As I hammered it in, it made a sharp, rising tone—also just right. After clipping the rope in, I suddenly felt much better. I told Warren what I'd done, and he said, "Sounds good. Go ahead."

Down on the ground, Rob was looking smaller. He waved and yelled up, "Looks wild!" I agreed but thought it might be a good idea to try out these new things closer to the ground.

Above me the corner looked a little easier. I climbed up about ten feet and began to feel the need for a second piton. I hammered in a horizontal. It made a dull, hollow sound as it went in and didn't feel as solid as the first one. I clipped in and went on until the corner suddenly got steeper, leaned to the right, and looked much harder.

"You might want to traverse out onto the face there," Warren said.

I could see his point. A series of tiny, ledge-like holds ran across the smooth face to the right. Protection was definitely called for. I needed another big angle but didn't have one. Instead, I found a small crack near the corner and hammered in a horizontal. After it was two-thirds of the way in, it starting making buzzing and twanging sounds and wouldn't go in any farther. It was the best I could do.

After clipping in, I stepped out onto the face and started edging across it, moving from one foothold to the next. This face climbing was much more enjoyable than the strange maneuvers I'd made below, but as I got farther from the corner—and my last piton—I became intensely aware of the empty air beneath my feet.

"Hey, Glen," Rob shouted up. "That looks great. But where are you going?" I heard laughter from down below and talking between Rob and Warren. Then Rob yelled, "What are you climbing on? Lichens?" More laughter.

But I was too busy to reply. I was at the end of the traverse, standing on a small ledge, trying to figure out what to do next. The ledge was about six inches long and two inches wide, comfortable for one foot at a time. Ten feet above me I could see some big holds that led to easy rock and a large ledge, the end of climb. My last challenge was to figure out how to climb those ten feet.

After a careful examination, I found a sequence of three footholds. A very small one for my right foot, then a tiny one above it for my left, and then a larger one for my right. If I could stand up on that third hold, I could reach the big holds above, and my problems would be over. But there was very little for the hands.

I rested a minute and wiped my fingers on my pants and on the rock, making sure they were quite dry. I wanted to cinch up my bootlaces but couldn't do it without falling off. If only I could get in a piton—but there were no cracks. That last piton looked very far away.

After taking several deep breaths, I placed my right foot carefully on the first hold and stood up on it. Next, I put my left foot on the tiny foothold, very precisely, and moved up on it. As I was raising my right foot to the third hold, I felt something shift in my left foot. I looked down and saw it all happen—in very clear, very slow motion: the edge of the boot sole bending and the tiny hold coming back into view and the boot sliding off. I saw my right foot going back down to the first hold, but too fast, glancing off and slipping past it. All my weight was on my fingertips, and I felt them straightening out. I saw my right foot hit the six-inch ledge. I tried to make it stay there, but too much weight was coming down. I saw the ankle bend outward and the foot slide off.

Instantly the rock was rushing past my face. I heard someone yell. The rope would catch me in a second. I felt a tug on my waist but it didn't slow me down. The top piton had pulled out. The rock was blurring past. I felt a second tug. It had no effect. Why wasn't the system working? Why had the rope broken? The ground was coming up with an incredible rush.

Then it stopped.

I was dangling on the rope twenty feet above the ground. Warren lowered me down. Rob came over with a startled look on his face. "Are you all right?" His eyes were wide with astonishment.

I seemed to be OK. I hadn't felt anything when Warren's belay stopped me. Due to stretch in the rope I had nearly hit the ground before it recoiled and left me hanging twenty feet up. The two pitons that had pulled out were still clipped to the rope, resting against my bowline. I stared back up the wall. The point I had fallen from looked shockingly far away.

Warren was still sitting in the tree, grinning down at me. "Not bad. A fifty-footer on your first fall. And done in perfect form. All the way down!" He curled his fingers into claws and put them on the rock. I looked at my fingertips. They were covered with blood. They had never given up trying to hold on.

I untied and walked over to the car. After washing off the blood and putting on some bandages, I sat down and thought about what had just happened. I should have been happy to be alive, but I was angry. Beginners' mistakes had let death come too close. I had to learn more. That climb couldn't defeat me. As soon as my fingers healed, I'd come back and finish that lead.

Warren was tired of sitting in that tree. "Anybody else?" he called down.

Rob wanted some action. He climbed up to the tree, and Warren took the lead. Rob went second, and I followed with a top rope. Despite my aching fingers, it was surprising how much easier it was when there was no need to worry about falling.

From the big ledge we scrambled down to the car and had some lunch. Warren said there was more good climbing on the wall, farther to the right. My fingers were throbbing, and I didn't feel like using them, but Warren said, "Don't worry. We'll do friction climbing. There won't be anything to hold on to."

We climbed up smooth slabs, wondering why we didn't fall off. Warren kept saying, "Trust your feet. Trust your feet." Rob complained about the blood I was leaving behind, making the rock slippery. I put on more bandages and added adhesive tape.

Warren pointed out cracks of various sizes and demonstrated the strange body positions needed to climb them. Finally, he showed us how to self-belay, sliding a prusik loop up a fixed line, and we scampered all over the place like lizards till the sun went down.

Then we picked out a flat spot next to the wall by a big pine tree. Warren and Rob walked back to the car and drove off to the Village Store for groceries while I gathered wood for a campfire. There were lots of dead branches on the ground. I broke them over my knee and jumped on the bigger ones after spanning them between two rocks. Soon I had a big pile of oak, pine, and manzanita. I scraped the leaves and pine needles away and started a fire on the white granite sand. It was roaring by the time they came back with dinner. Rob wrapped potatoes in tin foil and buried them in the sand. I spread the fire out over them, and we waited for it to burn down to a bed of coals. Warren opened a jug of Red Mountain wine and we passed it around.

He took off his shoes and stretched out by the fire. "Yeah, you should get yourself some of these rock shoes," he said, wiggling his toes. "They're hard on the toes, but they make you look good on the rocks." He laughed. "That was quite a fall, one of the best I've ever seen. You'll go far in this business, young man, up—or down!"

My fall reminded him of one he had taken on El Capitan when he was nailing up the right side of Boot Flake, a fifty-foot expanding crack: "I was close to the top of the flake, placing a final pin. I was going to hit it one more time. I had the hammer back, and when I struck the blow I hit the first pin I'd placed at the bottom of the flake!" He was laughing and waving his hammer hand in the air. "I swear the fall was that fast. The pitons had forced the crack wider, and they popped out as I fell, one after the other. And there I was back at the beginning, looking at that last pin I'd been hitting, way up there by itself. All the pins that came out were stacked up on the rope at my tie-in, in perfect order, so it didn't take long to get back up there."

I wanted to hear more about El Cap, so I told Warren about how I'd walked up to the base with Rich Calderwood, during the final push, and watched him prusik up the fixed ropes with a duffel bag of supplies dangling from his waist.

Warren said doing it that way was a ton of slow, hard work. They had tried other methods that didn't work out, such as the Dolt Cart.

"There was a big ledge, twelve hundred feet up, and we thought it would be great if we could haul loads up to it in one pull. So Dolt—he actually was an engineer—made a winch and installed it on the ledge. Then he made a special cart and put bicycle wheels on it to reduce the friction as the load went up the wall.

"Dolt loaded up the cart on the ground. Powell and I were on the ledge, winching and winching and getting arm weary. We had built up a huge pile of rope on the ledge and decided to look over the edge and see where the cart was. We couldn't see it. So we yelled down to Dolt, 'Where's the cart?' He yelled back, 'It's still on the ground!' We had just been getting the stretch out of the rope and we were pooped already, so we had to think of something else."

We passed the jug while Warren talked.

"Dolt was a wonderfully crazy character," he continued. "We named that ledge after him—Dolt Tower. It was almost Dolt Memorial Tower. The rappelling we did was pretty wild: two-hundred-foot drops on one strand of rope over huge exposure. So we always rappelled with a prusik safety knot on the rope, just in case something went wrong. One time Dolt had just started the rappel down from the Tower. He was out of sight when I heard a horrible screech, and I thought, 'That's it. He's a goner.' I looked over the edge, expecting to see a tiny body flying down the wall. But Dolt was only twenty feet away, with an agonized look on his face. His beard was caught in the prusik knot! He trimmed it short after that."

By now the fire had become a bed of glowing embers. Warren spread them out evenly with a stick and laid T-bone steaks directly on them. While the steaks sizzled, I dug out the potatoes, sliced them with my pocket knife, and buttered them with a horizontal piton. The steaks were flipped onto their other side for a minute, then plucked off the coals with the knife point, scraped clean of ashes, and laid on a flake of granite to cool. We picked them up in our hands and wolfed them down, with growls of satisfaction.

Then we leaned back against the wall, passed the jug around, and watched the firelight flickering on the tree trunks and the boulders. The air had gotten chilly, but the fire kept us warm on one side, and the granite wall at our backs still held the heat of the day. The day was over, but we didn't feel like going home.

Royal Arches and Half Dome, circa 1950. Photograph by Ansel Adams.

2
Royal Arches

That first summer in the Valley, Rob McKnight and I did some climbs with experts and learned how it was done. After that, it was time for us to launch out and do a long, serious climb on our own.

We chose the Royal Arches. This route ascended an impressive, smooth-looking wall, following a long sequence of cracks and ledges. The 1954 guidebook said it "provided all the varieties and difficulties of climbing technique" and was definitely an all-day climb, especially for a group of beginners.

Rob's best friend, Frank Gronberg, wanted to come with us. They had grown up in small towns near Chicago and met at the University of Illinois. Their vacations were spent canoeing long rivers and spelunking. College became tiresome, and they decided to explore caves in the Yucatan. On the way they stopped in New Orleans. It was Mardi Gras, and a week of heavy indulgence changed their plans. Now they wanted to see the Wild West and climb some mountains. They hitchhiked across the Southwest to California and reached Yosemite. Frank worked in the Yosemite Lodge kitchen, Rob still ran the dishwashing machine, and I had been promoted from busboy to bellhop. The tips were good and enabled me to buy some pitons and other gear from the Ski Hut in Berkeley.

Unfortunately, Frank hadn't done any roped climbing, just some bouldering. I asked Rob if this would be a problem. "No," he said. "He's tough. You can count on him. If he decides to do something, he won't give up."

On our next day off we packed up our gear and, after breakfast at the Lodge cafeteria, headed up the Valley toward the Arches. Rob was wearing a beret, cocked at a jaunty angle. He had picked it up in San Francisco, wanting to look like a beatnik.

Of medium height and well built, he was a natural athlete, and this got him into trouble. His large, round eyes expressed enthusiasm for each new experience. Whenever he reached a ledge, he would look up at the next wall and want to climb it directly. He didn't have the patience to look around the corner for something more reasonable.

Rob was carrying our two coiled ropes crisscrossed over his chest like the bandoliers of cartridges worn by Pancho Villa. He had just bought a hammer holster, and as we walked along the road, whenever he saw a squirrel or chipmunk he would quick-draw his hammer and go "Pow! Pow!"—as fast as Jack Palance in *Shane.*

Up ahead we could see our wall, gleaming in the morning sunlight. "Holy smokes!" Rob exclaimed. "Look at that. This is going to be great."

Frank didn't say much. Perhaps he was wondering about what he had gotten himself into. Up till now, they had been sharing their adventures, but Rob had been bragging about all the great climbs he had been doing, and Frank didn't want to get left behind.

Rob and I would do the leading, so Frank's job was carrying the baggage. He had been to the war surplus store in Merced and bought a backpack for two dollars. It was made of heavy canvas with a camouflage pattern. It had an awkward, boxy shape that stuck out too far, and I wondered what it had been designed to carry. The pack was filled with our food, extra clothes, and army ponchos in case of rain, so he had to wear an ammo belt with two one-quart army canteens dangling from it.

His final piece of impedimenta was a two-quart desert canteen. This was a round metal canteen with flattened sides that were covered with blanket fabric for insulation. He carried it by a strap worn over the shoulder and across the chest. During their hitchhike across the southwestern United States, they had spent many hours standing on the shoulders of highways, broiling in the sun, waiting for the next ride. Frank had become very attached to that canteen and what it carried. Later, in the Valley, Warren Harding noticed this and gave him his nickname—Desert Frank. Long and lean, with narrow prospector's eyes, Frank at age twenty-one looked as if he had already spent a long time in the desert.

We took the horse trail past The Ahwahnee hotel and then scrambled up a short slope to the base of the wall. We roped up and Rob laughed when he remembered the comic way Harding had shown us how to tie in. Now we felt like veterans.

Rob did some stretching exercises to loosen up, and Frank chuckled, "Hey, bud, this isn't a football game."

"That's right," Rob shot back, "it's much bigger than that. This game lasts all day. It isn't over till the sun goes down."

He lectured Frank on the importance of not stepping on the rope, because it might get cut on the sharp edges of the rocks. With three hundred feet of rope on the ground, you had to step carefully.

The first pitch was an easy-looking low-angle chimney, but the rock had been polished quite smooth by the glaciers and it was slippery. I led up, placing a runner around a chockstone. Above that I came to a fixed piton and felt rather superior when I decided that I didn't need to clip into it.

Another chockstone blocked the top of the chimney. I moved out under it, grabbed its top, and swung up onto a good ledge. After anchoring in, I pulled up the rope and could hear them talking below.

"OK," Frank shouted up to me.

"OK what?" Rob said to him.

"I'm starting. Pull up the rope."

"You're supposed to say 'up rope.'"

"Up rope, dammit!"

Frank had a hard time in the slippery chimney. His baggage got in the way, and to get good cross-pressure he had to switch the pack around and wear it on his chest.

Above the chimney we climbed several rope lengths up a sequence of exfoliation steps and ledges, trending to the right. The climbing varied from class 3 to class 5 and wasn't very hard. We were making good progress, and I could hear Rob humming lines from "Stout-Hearted Men."

After the last step we came to a big, sandy ledge, with a smooth wall rising above. A few cracks ran up it here and there, offering various possibilities. Rob liked the first one he saw. Twenty feet of polished rock led up to a small tree. Above it, two cracks or grooves went directly up the wall and then started diverging. It was Rob's turn to lead.

"This looks challenging," he said. "I want to do it."

I walked fifty feet to the right and found a crack that looked easier, but Rob wasn't interested. He wanted to push his limits and do something impressive. I pointed out that it would be OK until the grooves diverged, but then what?

"It'll be OK," he said. "I'll find something."

I put him on belay. Rob climbed up to the tree and placed a runner around it.

"What about going right there? How does that look?" I asked.

"I want to do it direct. Straight up."

Frank shook his head doubtfully. He'd seen this attitude before.

Then, with his left hand and foot in one groove, right hand and foot in the other, Rob stemmed up the wall. After twenty feet he placed a piton and continued up. The cracks started to diverge, and after ten more feet he was spread-eagled between them, flat against the rock, and breathing hard.

He needed to shift to one groove, and chose the right-hand one. He got his left hand into it, but when he moved his left foot he lost too much support and fell with a curse and a clatter of hardware. The piton held, and I lowered him to the ledge.

Frank rushed over and asked if he was all right. Rob rubbed a scraped elbow and said he was fine. Frank gave him a big drink of water from the desert canteen. It was clear that everything was OK, and Frank couldn't resist the opportunity.

"Great performance," he said with a grin. "I can see you're really good at this."

Rob glared at him for a moment, but his irrepressible smile returned. "You didn't let me warm up enough."

I took the lead and climbed up to the tree, interested in what was on the right. After untying, I pulled the rope through Rob's piton and tied back in. We could retrieve the piton and carabiner from above, after the pitch was finished.

From the tree I traversed right into a shallow bowl. It was hard to find enough holds in the steep, smooth rock, but a good piton crack promised security. I climbed up and placed a pin. After ten more feet of delicate face climbing, the angle eased back, and a long run-out ended at a ledge with a large Douglas-fir on it. Deep grooves had been cut into its bark by people pulling down rappel ropes. I anchored to it and called down for my partners to come up. Frank was wearing army boots he had gotten from the store in Merced. They had been made for tough terrain but not for climbing. The soles stuck out from the uppers and rolled off small holds, and Frank was grumbling about it.

Rob was belaying him and called down, "You can ask for tension if you need it. Don't be embarrassed." He gave me a knowing wink. "It's nothing a beginner should be ashamed of."

"Just up rope, dammit, and keep it out of my face."

After comments like that, there was no way Desert Frank would ask for help from the rope. His baggage made it worse. I could hear the desert canteen bonking against the rock as he moved up. He got to the ledge without using any tension, and I think Rob was a little disappointed.

"You did good," he said, "but don't step on the rope."

"All right, all right. I've got eyes, you know."

After retrieving the piton and carabiner, we continued up the wall. The climbing was excellent, up a long series of slabs, cracks, and flakes, some sharp, some rounded, all very solid. It was a pleasure to look up at the rock and see the answers quickly, using the holds lightly and without fear. There seemed to be a comfortable ledge with an anchor tree every hundred feet. The leaves and pine needles were bright green against a deep blue sky. The rock was smooth and white, with black speckles from lichen and minerals.

I enjoyed sitting on the ledges with my feet dangling off. As we gained height, everything on the Valley floor got smaller, and the snowy peaks of the high country started coming into view. To the west I couldn't see Lower Yosemite Fall, but a cloud of mist was coming out of its alcove in rainbow colors: red, orange, green, and blue.

We continued up the crack system until it ended at a blank wall. At this point the route traversed two hundred feet to the left, before reaching another crack system that led up to the Valley rim. The problem was that fifteen feet of blank rock separated us from the start of the traverse ledge.

This was the famous Pendulum Pitch. From the top ledge I climbed up twenty feet to two fixed pitons driven up under a flake. I clipped in and Rob lowered me back down. Then, suspended on the rope, I started walking across the wall, trying to reach the traverse ledge, which at its start was only one inch wide.

After a few steps it was obvious I was too high. Rob gave me more rope, and I tried again, leaning left and reaching for the ledge. But I leaned too far, my feet slipped, and I skidded back to where I started. Rob lowered me a few feet more, and this time, just before slipping, I grabbed the ledge with my left hand, asked for slack, pulled up, and stood on the ledge.

It got wider as I went left, and soon I found a good belay spot. Frank came next. Then Rob climbed up, substituted a runner for the carabiner, stepped across, untied, and pulled the rope through. We traversed farther and came to a good spot for lunch about halfway between the Pendulum and the Rotten Log—the next famous pitch.

We sat on the ledge and looked down. Rob and I had been this far off the ground before but only on climbs like Arrowhead Spire, where you scrambled up talus and brush for a thousand feet before reaching the last few hundred feet of clean, sculpted rock. But this cliff went all the way down to the Valley floor, smooth and sleek.

"This is it," Rob said. "The real thing."

We'd done ten rope lengths to get here. For the first time it felt like we were in the middle of a big wall.

It was hot on the ledge. There was no escape from the sun. The roll of Life Savers in my pocket was used up. I took a drink and pushed the water around in my mouth with my tongue, rinsing off the sticky layer of thirst scum that had been building up. Our two one-quart canteens were empty, and the desert canteen was half empty.

A thousand feet below we could see tourists floating down the river on inner tubes and air mattresses. They had a million gallons of water but didn't appreciate it. They just rubbed suntan lotion on each other and basted like turkeys.

Frank dug into the pack and got out the food. I had brought salami and crackers. The crackers had broken into little pieces, and the salami was sweating inside its wrapper from the heat that had penetrated the pack. I gnawed at the salami and munched the cracker crumbs. Each bite took longer and longer to chew and swallow, and I kept wanting to drink more water but knew I shouldn't.

Rob and Frank had two cans of sardines. Rob had traded a piton for them with someone in Camp 4. The wrappers and keys were missing, and he had forgotten to bring a can opener.

"Don't look at me. You said you'd take care of everything, Mr. Expert."

"No sweat," Rob said. "Watch this."

He took a horizontal piton off the hardware sling and put one of the cans on the ledge. Placing the piton point on the can, he gave it a sharp rap with his hammer. The can dented in. He hit it again, and a yellow fluid oozed out around the point of the piton.

"What's that?" Frank asked.

"Mustard sauce. It's sardines in mustard sauce."

Rob moved the piton and hit it again, trying to make an incision around the lid, but the piton was dull and only inflicted small wounds. Under his blows the lid mashed in, and more of the thick yellow fluid squirted out of the holes like toothpaste, with bits of sardine in it.

"God. That's disgusting," said Frank.

"Now, now. Don't be squeamish. That's our lunch. You've got to eat and keep your strength up if you want to be a rock smasher."

Rob found a piton with a thinner blade and sharper edge. He cornered the battered, misshapen can between his foot and the rock wall. Holding the piton parallel to the ledge, he inserted the point and tapped the piton along sideways, like a chisel. After cutting halfway around the lid, he pried it open.

We looked inside. Little mangled fish bodies were floating in the yellow fluid.

"It looks like vomit," Frank said. "Throw it away."

Using the piton like a spoon, Rob scooped out the sardines and chewed them slowly, with delight. After slurping up the rest of the sauce, he wiped the last bits of sardine fins and mustard off his lips and smiled.

"Outstanding!" he said with a burp. "Pass the canteen, please."

"What's in the other can?"

"Sardines. In tomato sauce."

"Christ. That's even worse. I'll eat some gorp."

They finished their lunch in silence.

Rob leaned back and dozed off. Frank was wide awake, wondering what would happen next. He'd never been so far off the ground before. I could see it was bothering him, just like it did me the first time. But Desert Frank would not give in to it. He just sat there calmly, took another swig from his desert canteen, and tried to look like he wanted to be here.

Some of our pitons were bent from the hammering. I spread them out on the ledge and banged them back into shape. Then I looked up and saw that the sun was getting too close to the horizon. It was time to get back into action.

We continued the traverse and came to the second pendulum. I climbed up forty feet, clipped into a runner around a tree, and Rob lowered me down. This traverse was easier than the first one. Dangling on the rope, I walked across twenty feet of blank rock, climbed up a crack, and arrived at the base of the Rotten Log. This was an old tree, shaped like a ship's mast, which had died, fallen, and now leaned over a chasm. After climbing it, you regained the rock at the top and continued up the route.

The alternative to this was a right-facing open book known as the Rotten Log Bypass. It was steep and had an overhang at the top. Of course, Rob wanted to climb it.

"I didn't come up here to climb a tree," he said. "I can do that in Chicago. Pratt told me about this pitch. He likes it."

The problem with that was Chuck Pratt often liked pitches other people wanted to avoid. But the cracks looked good. If Rob put in enough protection, the fall wouldn't be too long.

He climbed up twenty feet and hammered in a piton. After ten more feet he placed another one.

"Here's the hard part," he said. "It's a lieback. A steep one."

"How good are your pitons?"

"They're very good."

"OK. Go for it."

It was a strenuous sequence of liebacking and face-climbing moves. After twenty feet he came to the overhang, which had no obvious weaknesses. He tried reaching up over it but couldn't find any holds. Traversing to the right was no better. Then he looked back left and saw a horn of rock sticking out from the left-hand wall. He got his left foot up on it. Using it for cross-pressure, he found a new hold for his right foot, moved up, and feverishly searched for handholds above the overhang. At last he found something, pulled up, and disappeared from sight with a whoop of triumph.

As I followed the pitch, Rob started shouting down, "Hurry up. Hurry up."

"Why?"

"Ants."

"What?"

"Ants! Marabunta!!"

I was at the overhang and couldn't go fast.

"Are you near a piton?"

"Yes."

"Tie into it. I've got to take you off belay. I'm getting out of here!"

This was very odd. I anchored to the pin and waited. After a few minutes he put me back on belay, and his voice sounded farther away. When I got to his first ledge I saw the problem. It was swarming with ants, reminding me of the army ants in *The Naked Jungle.* I crossed the ledge in quick steps and must have crushed hundreds of them.

When I reached Rob's new ledge, I congratulated him on his fine lead. It had put him in a happy mood. Impulsively, he grabbed my arm and gave me a wild-eyed stare.

"Marabunta!" he said. "Already they've reached California. We'll have to move farther north."

Rob scratched at his ant bites as I belayed Frank up. The sun was nearing the horizon as we climbed several pitches straight up. Then we started trending left toward the Jungle, a dense thicket of trees and bushes perched on a steep slab just below the Valley rim. A big overhang jutted out above it.

"How are we going to get over that?" Frank asked.

I was wondering the same thing. The guidebook didn't say anything about it, so there had to be some way around it, but I couldn't see the answer.

Lights were coming on in the Valley as we reached the final problem, a long friction traverse into the Jungle. Rob led across it to an island of rubble and put a sling around a small boulder. When I got there I thought his anchor looked insecure, so I tapped in a piton under the boulder. Not much better, but it would have to do. To the left, sixty feet of smooth friction slab separated us from the Jungle.

It was getting dark as I started across. There were no holds, and no protection. I kept telling myself not to lean in, or my feet would slip. Some pine needles had fallen onto the slab from tall trees in the Jungle. Before each move I brushed the rock carefully with my left hand. If I stepped on a bundle of pine needles, they would slip and I would fall. As I neared the Jungle I wanted to go faster and get it over with, but I told myself to go slower. I was fifty feet from Rob, and a fall might drop me off the slab and leave me dangling under the overhang below.

Finally, I reached out, found a branch I thought I could trust, and pulled myself into the Jungle. Brush had never felt so good. I anchored to a tree and belayed Rob across. Then it was Frank's turn.

It was quite dark now. Desert Frank had never done a traverse like this. It was a new kind of problem for him to solve, and he couldn't even see it. As he came across, Rob said, "Go slow. Stick your butt out. Trust your feet."

I couldn't see him, but I could hear him muttering, "Jeez Crize. Jeez Crize," as the desert canteen bonked on the slab with a hollow sound. It was empty now.

At last he reached us, and we were safe. But what next? Dense vegetation shut out the starlight, and we couldn't see a thing. There had to be an answer to the overhang problem, but in the darkness we wouldn't be able to see it. The best answer was to stay where we were. Everything would be clear in the morning.

We could hear a faint trickle of water. After digging down through rotting vegetation and mud, we found some moisture and started slurping and snuffling like hogs at the trough. The water was slimy and moldy, and full of things that made us gag and cough. Perhaps it was good that we couldn't see them. But at least it was water—sort of.

The best places to spend the night were on the uphill sides of the trees, where leaves and pine needles had piled up and made a rounded saddle. The surface was soft but slippery, so we tied into the trunks. Rob and Frank found usable trees a few yards up the slope.

It was a strange place to spend the night. I sat on my saddle of pine needles and leaned back against the tree. The air was filled with the perfume of azalea blossoms that I couldn't see, and for a long time I played "Scheherazade" in my head.

The night took forever to pass, but when I could see the white blossoms I knew there would be another day. As it got light I could see the rope running uphill through bushes to a cedar. Rob stuck his head out. His face was streaked with mud from the water-snuffling. He looked down at me.

"Mornin' blues," he said.

"What?"

"Mornin' blues. That's what we say in Chicago, in the mornin'."

Farther up the slope I heard Frank digging for more water. Then I heard him coughing and spluttering.

"Let's get the hell out of here," he shouted.

We gathered at Rob's tree and coiled the ropes, which had become a tangled mess during the night. "Don't step on the ropes," Rob said.

"It doesn't matter when they're on a heap of pine needles, for Christ's sake," Desert Frank shot back.

Breakfast didn't take very long, since there was nothing to eat. Some scarred bushes and bent grass led up to the left, forming a faint path. We hadn't been able to see these signs in the dark. At the end of the Jungle we came to some class 3 rock, at the base of the overhang. As we traversed left, the overhang got smaller, and after two hundred feet we came to a break in the cliff, scrambled to the top, and shook hands.

What a pure pleasure it was, walking along the Valley rim, hands in pockets, free and easy. We passed the summit of Washington Column, descended North Dome Gully to the Valley floor, and a few minutes later I was looking up at the wall we had just climbed. It was satisfyingly smooth and steep. The place where we had eaten lunch looked quite blank, but yesterday we had enjoyed sitting there, suspended in space.

"Hey, we're real rock smashers now," Rob said with a big grin. "That was great. What's next?"

The hardware jingled as we walked on through the forest. Up ahead the Lost Arrow and Yosemite Point Buttress were gleaming in the morning sunlight.

East Face of Mount Whitney. Photograph by Eric Tressler.

3

One Day
on Whitney

It was August and the Valley was hot and dusty. Camp 4 was overflowing with tourists, and it was time to get some fresh air in the high country. In Hervey Voge's *The Climber's Guide to the High Sierra*, I found places with intriguing names like the Minarets, the Palisades, and the Sawtooth Ridge. The photographs and drawings of them were compelling. These were alpine peaks, like the mountains where climbing had begun over a century ago.

The highest peak in the Sierra was Mount Whitney, toward the southern end of the range. At 14,495 feet, it was also the highest peak in the forty-eight states, and that gave it a special appeal. A trail led to its top from the east side, but the interesting thing for climbers was its east face. In photographs the face was quite impressive, and a famous route went up it. The guide said there were only a few class 5 pitches on it; the rest was easier. I asked some friends about this and they agreed, saying that for Yosemite climbers it was easy, but the location and quality of the rock made it a classic.

When I told Rob McKnight about it, his eyes opened wide with excitement. For a kid from Chicago this would be the Wild West, with altitude! By working overtime, we talked our boss into giving us two and a half days off. This would be just enough. It would take half a day to get to the town of Lone Pine and the trailhead. We would hike up to Whitney on the second day, then climb it, descend, and drive back on the third day.

This was going to be a big trip for my old 1950 Chevy Coupe, so I gave it a careful checkup. Then, early one afternoon, we threw our stuff into the car and took off.

Tuolumne Meadows was refreshing, but it looked kind of tame compared to where we were going. I drove up to Tioga Pass, down to Lee Vining, turned right onto Highway 395, and the adventure began. I'd never been on the east side of the Sierra before. Everything would be new.

We took the two-lane blacktop, heading south across sage flats and through groves of forest. At first the mountains of the Sierra crest were not very inspiring, but then two fine peaks appeared, with pointed summits and steep walls with glaciers at their base. This was what we had come for. From photographs, I knew these peaks must be Banner and Ritter. They disappeared as we went through more forest and came out onto another sage flat. Rob was in the passenger seat, taking it all in.

Suddenly he exclaimed, "Holy cow! Look at that!" I looked back to the right and saw a dramatic line of pinnacles silhouetted against the sky, like a row of giant fingers.

"Must be the Minarets!" I pulled over onto the shoulder, got out, braced my elbows on the roof of the car, and looked at them through binoculars. Instinctively, I wanted to be up there.

It was time to get busy with the guidebook, so we traded places. Rob drove on and we passed by a towering, pointed peak with a big rock wall near the road to Convict Lake. "That's Mount Morrison," I said. Rob kept weaving back and forth across the dotted line on the road as he tried to see the mountains I was describing.

Farther on I saw some peaks that might have been part of the Palisades. After that the Sierra crest got less interesting, but I knew there were many fine places hidden behind it. By now it was late afternoon, and as we drove through Owens Valley great blue shadows from the peaks were advancing across the highway.

After passing through several small towns we reached Lone Pine and stopped at a hamburger stand. We ordered burgers, fries, and milkshakes for dinner and sat outside. The food was good, but the real feast was for the eyes: a superb composition of pointed summits, serrated ridges, and sheer walls, all made of pure white granite. It was easy to pick out Whitney by the distinctive shapes of two tooth-like summits just to its left—Keeler and Day needles. Through my binoculars the east face looked like a big Yosemite wall, and I wondered where our route went on it.

We drove up to Whitney Portal, where the road ended in a grove of Jeffrey pines. Granite walls rose above us, and Lone Pine Creek came cascading down smooth slabs. Now we were above eight thousand feet, and the air was cool and fresh.

The trail began at a huge boulder, at the very end of the road. There were two massive wooden signs, with deeply chiseled letters painted white. One gave the mileage and elevation gains to campsites along the trail to the summit of Mount Whitney. The other sign was for the John Muir Trail. It gave the distances to many fine-sounding places we hadn't been to—Evolution Valley, Silver Pass, Thousand Island Lake—and one we had: Yosemite Valley, over two hundred miles to the north.

I knew that the Whitney Trail went up the canyon to a pass on the Sierra crest, and then followed the crest north to the summit of Whitney. That was eleven miles, with an elevation gain of six thousand feet. The east face could be reached by ascending the next canyon to the north. It had no trail and ended at East Face Lake,[1] just below the route. Climbers usually backpacked up this second canyon and camped at the lake. After climbing the face, they would descend a gully back to camp and hike out late on the second day—or the third, if the climb took too long.

We were full of energy and wanted to use our new powers to the fullest. After a summer of climbing and hiking, we were in great shape.

"Why don't we do the whole thing in one day?" I asked Rob. His eyes lit up instantly. He was willing to try anything, especially if it sounded a little bit crazy.

We would start at dawn and reach East Face Lake by noon. After eating lunch and taking a long rest, we would say to ourselves, "Now we start a new day." The climb was long but not hard. We should get to the top well before dark, and then take the trail back to the Portal. That could be done in the dark, if necessary, with a flashlight.

As we were discussing this, four men came clomping down the trail and dropped their heavy backpacks by the signs. They had just done the East Face, and we were a bit awed. These were the first real mountaineers we had seen; they were wearing knickers, Pendleton shirts, and alpine hats covered with pins that showed all the climbing clubs they belonged to and the famous mountains they had climbed. I was especially impressed by their big, heavy alpine boots, ice axes, and crampons, because we had none of those things.

I said we wanted to climb the East Face, too, and asked what it was like. They said it was a very long and very serious ascent and asked how many years' experience we had doing such things.

"We started climbing this year," I said.

Their leader raised his eyebrows skeptically.

"So it'll be just the two of you?" he asked. "What if you have an accident? Where is your margin of safety?"

I didn't have an answer for that. I just thought we were good enough because we had done harder climbs in the Valley.

"So, you'll take two ropes, in case you have to retreat?"

"Just one." Two would weigh too much.

"What if a storm comes in?"

That was a valid question, but we'd survived thunderstorms in the Valley in just our T-shirts.

"It's not like Yosemite up there, you know. It's fourteen thousand feet. It could be snow and ice instead of rain. And speaking of ice, you'll need ice axes for descending the Mountaineer's Route. It was a big winter, and there's still a lot of icy snow in the gully."

"We're not going that way. We'll descend the trail."

"But what about your camp? How will you retrieve it?"

"We won't have a camp. We'll do the round-trip in one day."

His eyebrows went up again. He looked at his partners and chuckled. "Well, good luck, boys. You're going to need it."

As they walked down the road I could hear them laughing about our presumption, and how they would be reading about our rescue in the newspapers.

Rob and I found a campsite with a view of the peak and sorted our equipment.

"How many pitons?"

"Ten. From a short, thin horizontal to a one-inch angle. No need for anything special."

"Let's make it five."

"What? Look at that wall. Be serious."

"I am serious. We can't take any extra weight on this one. Besides, I've heard there are some fixed pitons."

"What if someone from the Valley just cleaned them all out?"

"OK. Let's make it eight."

The ritual continued. Carabiners, hammers, runners, and a rope were added to the pile. Food: PayDay candy bars for energy, Life Savers for thirst, sardines and crackers and Wyler's Lemonade for lunch at the lake. And two one-quart water bottles. Our only luxury was two oranges.

We didn't have much in the way of clothes. All the money had gone into equipment. Our Valley clothes would have to do: T-shirts for sunshine, sweatshirts for cold, and Frisco jeans for everything. Our pants were full of holes, which had been patched over, but by now the patches had holes, too. Our thin, beat-up rock shoes weren't much better. They had been resoled, but now the rubber lugs were worn smooth again. Rob looked at the toe of his right shoe, where his sock poked through. He gave it a thoughtful wiggle.

We took nothing waterproof. Army ponchos would add too much weight and bulk. If we got caught in a storm, the key thing was to keep moving—up or down. That way you wouldn't freeze up. Just get out of there and leave the storm behind.

I picked a spot where I could see the mountain, took off my shoes, and crawled into the sack. I tried to sleep but my mind kept running over the list. Had we forgotten anything? I took comfort in the thought that, since our outfit was so simple, it would be obvious if anything was missing. Other things would be decisive: Distance. Altitude. Weather. Endurance.

✦   ✦   ✦

At first light I looked at the east face and watched the colors change until it was bathed in the orange light of sunrise. We got up, ate breakfast, said nothing, and hit the trail.

From the giant boulder we followed switchbacks up to the horse trail, then went right a short distance to the North Fork of Lone Pine Creek. A faint footpath led up its left side, through the forest. Soon the path disappeared in a field of huge boulders, and it was slow going finding a way over and around them. After that the canyon walls closed in, and the creek came down a slot choked with willows. There was supposed to be a ledge system on the right-hand wall that avoided the willows, but we didn't find it. So we thrashed our way up through the jungle, following the skinned and broken branches left by earlier climbers. The willows were so thick that at times the only passage was up the streambed itself. We sloshed up the cascading creek, pulling on the branches that surrounded it.

Then the canyon opened up, and we came to an idyllic tarn with a meadow and a grove of foxtail pines. We took a rest in the shade of the trees and laid our shoes and socks out in the sun to dry. To the west, the east face of Whitney towered above some intervening crags. It was getting closer.

We continued up the left side of the creek, ascended a talus slope, and entered another willow jungle. It looked like an endless struggle, but through a small opening I spotted some clean slabs on the other side of the creek. After a search I found a crossing, and the problem was solved. I took a drink from the creek, washed off my sweaty face, neck, and arms in the cold water, and waited for Rob to appear.

Time passed, but there was no sign of him. I decided he must be going too far through the jungle, so I climbed up the slope to get a better view. I was hoping to see some willows moving farther upstream—that would tell me where he was. But nothing was moving. The willow jungle also extended up the opposite side of the canyon for hundreds of feet, ending at some slabs and a cascade. Below the cascade I saw some movement in the willows. It was probably a deer we had startled, or maybe a bear looking for berries. The willows kept moving as the creature moved up. Then it emerged at the start of the slabs. It was Rob!

I yelled and waved my shirt. At first he couldn't hear me because of the noise of the cascade. But he moved away from it, looking for a way up. Finally, he heard me and realized he was off-route and had to come down.

When he got back, his shirt and pants were torn, his face and hands were grimy, and willow leaves were stuck in his hair. Deep in the willows, he had come to the stream that descended from the cascade and thought it was the North Fork. He gave me a sheepish, lopsided grin and said, "Nice little cascade up there."

The open slabs led up the right side of the creek, and soon we came to East Face Lake, where we would have lunch. Despite our problems we had made pretty good time, and I thought about taking a swim in the lake to cool off after the hot approach.

But as we sat there I realized that something was wrong. The lake was surrounded by impressive walls, but none of them looked like Whitney. I knew that mountains could appear to change shape as your own position changed, but this difference was too big. And where were Keeler and Day needles? There was no sign of them.

This could not be East Face Lake, so where was it? There was a notch at the far end of the cirque. Perhaps you could see Whitney from there. But the climb up to the notch looked harder than anything mentioned in the guidebook. I scrambled up a knoll and looked around. To the south there appeared to be a higher, hanging valley. Maybe East Face Lake was up there. We backtracked a ways and climbed a steep talus slope, encouraged by the sight of footprints in the dirt made by Vibram soles, the kind climbers wore.

We entered the hanging valley, turned west, and there they were— Whitney, Keeler, and Day, looking unbelievably sheer and pure. They were very close now. I still could not see a feasible route on Whitney, but we trudged on up a hot, gravelly valley, believing in the guidebook. A high moraine blocked our view of the lake, but when we got to its top there was no lake. Where was the damn thing?

Off to the right I could see a stream cascading down a cliff band. Was it up there? We climbed the cliff band, entered an austere basin, and there it was, at last—East Face Lake. I picked out a boulder near the shore. It cast a small patch of shade and I sat down, trying to get most of my body into its shadow. Nearby, Rob did the same, and we sat there, munching sardines and crackers and drinking our lemonade.

The sun was hot, the air was still, and the silence was remarkable. Each sound—crinkling paper or a foot grinding in the sand—seemed unnaturally clear and crisp. A network of stone walls had been built next to the biggest boulders, to protect campers from the wind, but no one was home. It looked like the remains of an ancient civilization. The unruffled lake was surrounded by barren sandy slopes. It was more like the Sahara than the Sierra, except for the icebergs floating in the lake.

I looked up and saw a bold pillar of granite rising to the summit of Whitney, two thousand feet above. This pillar was the east buttress. To its left was the massive east face we'd been looking at during the approach. Somewhere between these features was the East Face Route. It didn't seem possible that the climb consisted of only a few easy class 5 pitches and that the rest was easier. But the guidebook was not a work of fiction.

Rob was throwing rocks into the lake, trying to hit an iceberg. It was too far away. He came crunching back across the granite sand to my boulder.

"Well?" he asked.

I knew what he meant.

"What time do you think it is?"

"Lots of time left," I said. That was the problem. It was too early to turn back. Not a cloud in the sky—we couldn't blame it on the weather. After coming all this way, we had to take a look. At least we ought to go up and look at the first pitch. There was no excuse for not doing that. Gradually I shamed myself into getting up.

We filled the water bottles, put on the day packs, and started up the talus. I began to feel better. The energy was still there, and it wanted to be used. I was going full steam by the time we reached the notch of the first tower.

We roped up and Rob put me on belay as I started climbing the first pitch. The sun was off the wall now and the air was cool. Cracks and holds gave the granite an edgy texture that felt good as I moved up. We were under way at last.

After fifty feet the cracks ended at a small ledge where I found an old fixed piton. The wall above looked blank, but a series of holds led across the wall to the left. This must be the Tower Traverse. I was now at the edge of the great east face. Below me, the wall dropped a sheer five hundred feet to the talus, and the sudden exposure was startling.

I tested the piton with my hammer. It was solid, and I clipped in the rope with a carabiner. I called down to Rob that the traverse looked OK. Then, with my left foot, I stepped out over space to the first foothold. My left hand searched across the wall and found a nubbin. I eased my weight onto my left foot, brought my right foot across, and stood up on the hold. The rope ran easily through the carabiner, giving a slight, reassuring tug at my waist, telling me that it was reasonable to be here.

I stepped across again. A strong afternoon updraft was coming up the wall, flapping my shirt and cooling my heels. I stepped again, and it felt like I was dancing on air.

After a few more moves, I came to a short chimney, climbed up it to a ledge, and hammered in a piton for an anchor. "On belay," I called down to Rob. He was out of sight below, and I got no answer. Perhaps it was because of the wind. I yelled louder but still got no answer.

This was an old problem we had learned to cope with. I started pulling in the extra rope. When it pulled tight on him, with repeated tugs Rob would know he should start climbing. I kept pulling in more rope but still felt no resistance.

Aha! I thought, he's feeling good now and having fun. On easy rock, where there was no danger of falling, we would often try to climb faster than the belayer could pull in the rope, just for the hell of it. At this rate we would be up the climb in no time! I kept pulling in the rope, expecting Rob to appear at the start of the traverse. Here came the rope and . . . here came the end of the rope. No Rob!

A great shouting came up from below. I yelled back. We couldn't understand a thing. Several minutes passed.

Then Rob's head slowly appeared at the start of the traverse. He moved up and stood on the ledge by the fixed piton—unroped. He gave me that lopsided smile and said, "I had to take a crap. When I got back the rope was gone."

All he could do was hold on to the piton and carabiner because the rope had fallen through and was resting on a foothold halfway across the traverse. We talked it over. This situation was not covered in the how-to book.

I thought about pulling in the rope and throwing the end back to Rob, but the wind had gotten stronger and might blow it the wrong direction, leaving him farther from safety than before.

Rob decided to be bold. The traverse actually wasn't very hard. It was the exposure that made it scary, but that could be taken care of with mind control. Of course, the gusts of wind might make you feel a little unsteady. It's the kind of thing you don't notice when you're tied in.

Rob wiped his hands on his pants to get rid of the sweat that had been collecting on his palms. He scraped his shoes on the ledge, and took one last look around, making sure no new solution had magically appeared. And then he committed himself to the traverse.

Very carefully, he stepped across to the first hold and stood on it. I watched, still holding on to the belay rope, remembering that I should *not* pull it in as he advanced.

He made two more moves and found a stance where he could let loose with one hand. He bent down and grabbed the end of the rope. I let out some slack and, with one hand, he tied a loose knot around his waist as best he could. After one more step he came to better footholds. Then, in delicate balance, leaning his forehead against the wall, he freed both hands and quickly tied a solid bowline.

"Madre! I live!" he exulted.

He quickly finished the traverse and charged up the chimney. We took a break and drank some water. The tension had made us thirsty. There was an awkward silence, and I wondered if we were still just beginners.

It went better after that. The climb took on a rhythm as we swung leads up the wall. First came the Washboard, named for its pattern of rounded horizontal ripples. It formed a long, sloping ramp that diagonaled up and left, leading farther out onto the east face. This gave us several hundred feet of enjoyable class 4 climbing that ended in an alcove with sheer walls above. Here, for the second time, the route traversed around a major problem. The answer lay on the left, where a short, steep wall led to a knife-edged crest. Another smooth wall rose above it; the only choice was to climb down the other side to a large ledge, which we followed into a big corner, like an open book, in the center of the face.

In corners like this, the usual answer was to climb the crack where the two walls met, but I could see that would be extremely difficult. The left wall looked easier, so I climbed up it, unsure of where to go next. I came to a steeper section and then noticed a thin ledge going out to the left, around a corner. I followed this and found myself over tremendous exposure, much greater than on the Tower Traverse. I also found two fixed ring angle pitons, so now I knew I was on the famous Fresh Air Traverse. I clipped in and made a long stretch to the left. Once again it felt like I was dancing on air. Several more moves took me to an exposed stance. A smooth wall was above me, and a fierce-looking chimney was to the left. The chimney looked too hard for this route, so I tried the wall.

I reached up and, unexpectedly, my right hand found a bucket hold. I stepped up, and my left hand found another bucket. It was wonderful climbing—easy, but the exposure made it exciting. Next I climbed partway up a chimney and then traversed right to a belay ledge. Rob soon joined me, raving about how good the climbing was.

We sat on the ledge with our feet dangling over, peeled our last orange, and took in our marvelous situation. We were perched in the middle of the sheer wall that had looked so impossible from Lone Pine. It felt like all our months of practice had pointed to this day.

But it was getting late. The air up here was much colder. The shadow of Whitney was creeping out toward Lone Pine, and we had to keep moving.

The next section was called the Grand Staircase, a sequence of big blocks and short walls. The guide said we should climb this and look for a narrow chimney or crack on the left. Rob was in the lead when he called down, "Here it is." I climbed up. It looked too hard, a real Yosemite slot, but Rob was hot to do it. He wriggled up, grunting and cursing, using all the technique he had learned in the Valley. When he reached the top, there was an ominous silence. Then he said, "This isn't it. It's worse above." He put a runner around a horn and rappelled down. Now it was really late.

We continued up the Staircase and came to its end: a blank wall with a steep crack on its left side. This had to be it. Rob anchored in, gave me the hardware sling, and I started up. It was a steep jam crack for my left arm and leg. I had placed one piton and was moving on when suddenly I heard a clattering of hardware and Rob yelling. I couldn't imagine what was happening and just held on; then it got quiet and I looked down.

Pitons and carabiners were scattered all over the ledge. Rob uncovered his head and stared at up at me, an astonished look on his face. The knot on the hardware sling had come untied, and all the hardware had fallen on him. Fortunately, I didn't need any more pitons. I finished the pitch, Rob collected the gear, and I belayed him up. Once again there was an awkward silence.

A cairn of small stones was on the ledge. I dug into it and found an old rusty Prince Albert tobacco tin. Inside were folded pieces of paper, browned and crumbling at the edges, and a short, blunt pencil. The register went back decades and contained many famous names. As I added ours to the list, I couldn't help wondering if they made mistakes, too.

Only a few hundred feet of easier rock remained. We climbed up, traversed right, and looked up. No need for the rope now. We surged up the final rocks and stood on the summit, freed from the wall at last.

A splendid panorama lay before us. Hundreds of mountains, blue and golden, were gleaming in the evening sunlight. They didn't stop; they just turned lighter colors and curved gradually out of sight.

But we had no time to enjoy it. The sun was close to the horizon, and we had to keep going. I could see the trail going south, just west of the jagged Sierra crest. Hikers were heading down, small dots in the distance. It was two and a half miles to Trail Crest Pass. From there, the trail descended east into the drainage of Lone Pine Creek, leading toward Whitney Portal.

We quickly swallowed the last of our food and water, and Rob got out the flashlight.

"Oh, no!" he said. "The batteries are dead!"

Earlier in the day, while we were rummaging in the pack, the switch had accidentally gotten turned on. Suddenly the sunset didn't look so pretty. It would be impossible to reach the Portal by dark, but we had to try. The lower we got, the less frost we would have to endure during the bivouac.

The combination of exhilaration and desperation put us in a wild state. We ran down the trail—no time left for walking—and dashed past the startled hikers a few minutes later. At Trail Crest I was dismayed to see that the trail went far out to the right on a talus slope, where an endless series of switchbacks seemed to take forever to reach the bottom of the basin. A dozen hikers were on the switchbacks, descending to their camps.

But straight below me, a scree slope dropped down to a long snowfield that ended on the floor of the basin. We were in a lather now, and I decided to go all out. We plunged down the scree to the snowfield. The surface of the snow was hard because it was late season. It would be unsafe to glissade without ice axes, so we pawed through the talus and found long, thin shards of rock. We sat on the snow and zoomed down, controlling our speed by digging in our granite daggers. The snow was hard and bumpy, and we arrived at the bottom a bit battered. But looking back up at what we had done, we felt a new surge of exhilaration. It had only taken a few minutes, and the hikers were still high above us on the switchbacks!

We jumped up, found the trail, and continued at high speed, past a lake where several tents were pitched. The trail switchbacked down into a grassy gully with a stream at the bottom and boulders and small cliffs rising above. Under the overhangs, hikers had built up stone walls for protection against the weather, leaving small openings that served as doors and windows. People were looking out of their doorways, talking to each other, and campfire smoke drifted out of some of the windows. It looked like a village of twentieth-century cliff dwellers.

A man was sprawled on the grass by the creek, relaxing after dinner and smoking a pipe. As we passed by, he called out, "Hey, where's your camp? It's getting late. Real late."

"We don't have one. We're going on to Whitney Portal," I said.

"What? You'll never make it. Not tonight. You better stay with us. There's room in our cave. You can roll up in a poncho."

I thanked him for the offer, and we kept on going. Nothing was going to stop us now. But, as we went on down the trail, I finally had to admit it really was getting dark. That didn't mean we had to stop. It meant we had to go faster.

We jogged down the rocky trail and then, at another series of switchbacks, charged straight down the mountainside, jumping from boulder to boulder, skidding down slabs on shoes and pants, taking crazy chances, leaping over one problem and landing in the middle of the next one.

At last the trail leveled out. That felt good, but it meant we would be going slower, so we started running one hundred steps, then walking a hundred to recover our breath, then running a hundred more. Over and over.

The trail kept crossing the stream and we were stumbling in the dark. It looked like we would have to stop, but the moon rose and saved us from a frosty bivouac. Now I could see bits of trail here and there, between the shadows of the trees. As the moon got higher, I could see more, and we were able to resume a steady pace.

Then the trail started switchbacking down a long slope of forest and brush. I could see a cluster of lights far below—it must be campfires at the Portal. I kept on going down, being careful not to trip on the big roots of the Jeffrey pines that snaked across the trail like pythons.

I hadn't seen Rob for quite a while. He'd stayed with me on the rough stuff, but on the dirt trail my long legs had left him behind. He could see the trail as well as I could, so I wasn't worried. Now that the end was in sight, I didn't want to break the long-striding rhythm I had settled into.

Then I started hearing strange sounds from high on the hillside. Something was crashing through the brush, coming straight down the slope. What was it—a boulder? I stood off to the side and waited. Suddenly the brush above the trail parted and Rob tumbled down the bank, landing in the trail.

"You long-legged bastard," he said with a big grin. "I caught you!"

We kept on going down the trail in the moonlight, watching the campfires getting closer. It was easy now. The tension was gone, and my satisfaction flowed out onto the evening air, like the aromas from the Jeffrey pines.

East Face of Washington Column

4

The Endless Night

Now I wasn't so sure. Dawn would come in a few hours, and then I would decide whether to go up or down. There was nothing to do but wait. I looked down from the ledge. A few lights were still on, scattered across the Valley floor. Thousands of people were asleep down there.

I checked my tie-in again. Warren and Chuck looked like they were sacked out in Camp 4. Their tie-ins were loose. If they rolled over in their sleep they might fall off the ledge before pulling tight on their anchors.

Sitting there on my end of the ledge, I tried to relax and make time pass. I closed my eyes and thought about faraway mountains. First I recalled the six great north faces in the Alps that Rébuffat had written about, the names of the climbers who had made the first ascents, and in what years. Then I went on to the eight-thousand-meter peaks of the Himalaya and the Karakoram. It took a while to remember all fourteen of them, but that was OK. There was plenty of time. I named them from west to east, adding which country had made the first ascent, and in what year. Two of them were still unclimbed—Dhaulagiri and Shishapangma.

After that, I went on to the other continents, naming the highest peaks in the major ranges. Then I came back to North America and thought about its ten highest mountains. I knew their names and tried to put them in order, from highest to lowest, but couldn't quite decide where the three Mexican volcanoes fit into the sequence. That was all right. It must be nearly dawn by now.

I pulled the watch out of my pocket. It said 1:00 a.m. Surely more time had passed than that! But the watch was fully wound and still ticking. I decided to wait a very long time before looking at it again.

My eyes closed once more, and I searched for something else to think about, something more peaceful. I had hiked the Muir Trail from Yosemite to Mount Whitney. Now I retraced it in my mind, remembering each of my campsites along its two-hundred-mile length. Then I recalled the sequence of passes and basins and lakes on the trail, from beginning to end, and the names of all the creeks and the rivers they flowed into. I pictured one of the camps and saw myself sitting before a fire, but I was asleep. I saw myself tipping forward. . . .

A shock snapped my eyes open and my hand clutched for the tie-in. Nothing had changed.

Then I saw a bright halo of light behind Half Dome. The sun was coming up at last. At first it was a cool, pale light, but its strength was growing steadily. I smiled and watched as it grew brighter. The night had taken forever, but now it was finished. The stars lost their glitter. A line of pine trees came into silhouette on the shoulder of Half Dome. The light intensity kept building and then—slowly and gracefully—the full moon rose up into the night sky.

Everything was bathed in a silvery light, but I was too disgusted to enjoy it. I pulled out the watch. It said 1:30. I stared at the watch hands in disbelief. They didn't seem to move at all.

I looked up at the moon and Half Dome and noticed that the distance between them had grown wider. In that moment I realized the watch was useless—it served no purpose up here. You climbed when it was light, and when it was dark you forgot about time until it was light again.

The watch hands weren't moving and the ticking was driving me crazy. I threw it off the ledge and saw a brief gleam in the moonlight as it tumbled down through space toward the ground.

Down in the Valley, everyone was still asleep. From Tenaya Creek, a faint sound of rapids floated up on the still night air. After lengthening my tie-in, I lay down on the ledge. I closed my eyes, didn't think about anything, and listened to the flowing water. . . .

✦ ✦ ✦

Warren sat up. He blinked and stared off into space. Gradually his eyes came into focus. The green water jug looked cool and refreshing in the morning light. During the night, Warren and Chuck had sat up several times to drink, and now it was half empty. Over the past few days, they had gotten badly dehydrated in the hot sun.

He took a long drink. Suddenly he lowered the jug and asked, "How much water did you bring up?"

"Four gallons. Including that one."

He leaned back and looked up the wall.

"That should be enough," he said, pausing and scratching his chin. "We won't be coming back to this ledge." He prodded Chuck and dug into the food bag.

"How long do you think it will take?" I asked.

"Two days. Maybe three. It's hard to tell how close we are to the summit. Lots of overhangs up there."

I turned and looked up the wall. Two hundred feet above us, a huge roof jutted out over our heads. A loop of rope dangled over it, swaying slowly back and forth. From its anchor point under the roof, the rope arced down, out, and then went up over the lip of the roof and out of sight. Two days earlier, from the ground, I'd seen them prusik up that rope, dangling in space, and it looked exciting. Now the thought of going up there was making me feel shaky and sick to my stomach.

Chuck sat up and yawned.

"Anybody see that big rat last night?" He laughed. "I hope he doesn't like to chew on nylon."

"Yeah," Warren said. "Check your prusik knots, too. He might like the salt from your hands." Warren was eating tuna, scraping it out of the can with a piton.

"Pass me some of that Red Mountain water," Chuck said. "I think this bottle improves the flavor." The label was still on the jug. He was alternating bites from a block of cheese and a stick of salami. "Now I can swallow this stuff."

I didn't feel like eating anything.

Warren stood up and started bustling around, stuffing things into bags and saying, "OK. Who's taking what? Everything goes up today." He sorted through a rack of hardware. Chuck and I transferred the water to empty metal canteens and gas cans of various sizes. The glass jugs were too fragile for further use.

Sunlight had been creeping down the wall and finally reached the ledge, but its warmth didn't make me feel any better.

Chuck sat back on the ledge with his legs crossed, smiling in the new sunshine. He raised an empty jug to his mouth and started blowing deep, mellow notes across the opening. He watched Warren start up the first rope.

Suddenly he shouted, "Harding! I won't put up with any more of this. I want the day off!"

Warren kept going, grinning as he slid his knots up the rope. He was used to such outbursts.

"Now, now, Chucklehead," he said in a soothing voice. "There's a nice slot up there, waiting for you. Smooth and overhanging, just the way you like it."

"I warn you." Chuck grabbed his hammer and waved it in the air. "There are limits to what a man can endure!"

Warren laughed again. He reached the end of the first rope, switched to the next one, and called down, "OK."

"Want to go next?" Chuck asked.

"You go ahead. I'd slow you down."

"Thanks for bringing all that water. Sure you can haul all this stuff?"

I didn't say anything, but I nodded yes.

"See you up there," he said.

Now I *had* to go up.

Chuck prusiked up the first rope, singing "Vaya con Dios" in a plaintive voice.

Warren started out under the roof, dangling over the void. His shadow, cast on the wall below, swung wildly across the face, back and forth, as he moved up.

Chuck saw this and started laughing. "Harding, come back. Before it's too late!"

But Warren loved being in places like that. He kept going, passed the lip of the roof, and disappeared from sight.

Moby Dick

5

Base of El Cap

We started down the trail to the car. The sounds grew fainter, and I called back one last time.

"See you back in camp."

"No. No. Nooooo! We're not coming back!"

We felt our way down the trail in the dark, reached the car, and looked back up. The great bulk of El Capitan blotted out most of the stars. Faint howls and bits of singing were drifting down from The Nose.

Early the next morning I walked over to Pratt's table, wondering what had happened. The door of his tent was open. There he was, asleep, with a slight smile on his face. He looked content. The demon had been exorcised.

Southwest Face of Mount Conness. Photograph by Evan Russel.

6

The Wall
of Conness

In midsummer Tuolumne Meadows was as fresh as the Valley in spring, and I often drove up there for a timberline ramble. From Cathedral Peak, I couldn't stop staring at the unclimbed southwest face of Mount Conness. In the morning it was muted by blue shadows, but in the afternoon sunlight it stood out like a smooth wall of pure white marble, remote and serene. Just before sunset it took on an orange glow that I could not resist.

I asked Harding if he was interested.

"You bet," he said.

He had been looking at it for a long time. There had been an attempt on the wall earlier that summer, and one of the climbers, Don Goodrich, had been fatally injured while leading the second pitch. We decided that a party of three was a good idea and asked Herb Swedlund to join us. If there was a serious accident, one man would rappel and establish an anchor. The second man would lower the injured climber to the new stance, then rappel, and the process would be repeated until the ground was reached.

We drove up to Tuolumne Meadows with our girlfriends, hoisted heavy packs, and hiked up to a good campsite at Young Lakes. This would serve as a base camp. The girls would stay there and watch our progress through binoculars. If there was an accident, we would wave white T-shirts or signal with a flashlight, and they would run out to the road and sound the alarm.

We left some reserve supplies at the lakes. Chief among them were two one-gallon jugs of Red Mountain wine. Warren insisted that, in order to maintain good morale in the climbing party, these essential supplies must not be opened until we returned from the mountain.

After repacking our loads, the three of us walked up through timberline forests and meadows, hopped over streams, and then scrambled up glacier-polished slabs into an austere horseshoe-shaped cirque. At the base of the wall we dropped our packs and looked up.

It certainly was a high-quality wall, steep and smooth, like a piece of Yosemite Valley transported to the crest of the Sierra. The first major problem was a hundred feet up, at what we called the Ski Tracks, where two parallel cracks, several feet apart, diagonaled up and right.

This was where the fatal accident had occurred. After two months we could still see bloodstains running down the wall. Pitons and slings were placed here and there, in cracks and hanging from flakes, evidence of desperate improvisations as the injured climber was lowered down. On the ground, a flat rock was covered with bloodstains that dripped down its sides. It looked like an altar for human sacrifice.

I'm not sure I got any sleep that night.

✦ ✦ ✦

In the morning we packed everything into two duffel bags and started up the wall in a somber mood. At the Ski Tracks we climbed very slowly and very carefully, traversing past a hole between the cracks where a loose block had come out, causing the accident. The blood streaks started there.

After the Ski Tracks we reached a crack system that shot up the face, and we settled into a routine, swinging leads up the wall. Hours passed, and at one point in the afternoon, I was sitting on a ledge with the hauling bags. A fixed rope ran up the wall past an overhang to where Warren and Herb were starting to work on the next pitch. I couldn't see them, but I could hear hammering and voices. They were in a cramped spot, so I stayed below until the pitch was finished.

It was going to take a while, so I settled in. The ledge was a foot wide, but it sloped downward. I clipped my aid slings into the anchor and put my feet in them so I wouldn't slide off. As I sat there it started to get hot. The sky was clear and there was no breeze. The white U-shaped cirque seemed to be gathering all the sun's rays, and waves of heat were rising up the wall. I could feel energy draining from my body and realized I had to eat something to keep my strength up. But the food had been heating up, too. The cheese had melted. Inside its cellophane wrapper it looked like a piece of white blubber floating in a puddle of orange urine. The chocolate bars looked like diarrhea, with lumps in it.

Even the water tasted bad. In those days, there weren't any big plastic bottles made for carrying water. Instead of heavy metal canteens, we were using oval-shaped plastic bladders bought at a war surplus store. We called them "Shmoos," after the comic-strip creatures created by Al Capp. Each could hold five and a half quarts, and had a long neck and closure at one end. They were designed to contain human waste during trench warfare when there was no room for latrines. After baking in the heat, the thick, soft plastic—meant for other purposes—was giving the water a foul flavor.

The heat continued to build up. I put a windbreaker over my head to escape the sun, but sweat started trickling into my eyes.

From above the overhang I could hear hammering, shouts, and curses of frustration. They were struggling with a long, off-width crack. The leader would nest two stove-leg pitons for aid, step up, and nest two more. But he only had four, so he would drill a bolt, descend, and remove the pins, re-ascend, and repeat the process—over and over.

As time passed, the cirque became an oven. I sat there baking in the sun, like a piece of raw meat slowly turning into a strip of jerky. How I envied all those people down in Tuolumne Meadows—they could just walk over into the shade anytime they wanted to.

Then I saw the answer. Off to one side I noticed a tight chimney that was shady inside. I put prusik knots on the rope and swung across the wall into the slot. It was the loveliest tight chimney I'd ever met, blessedly cool and dark inside, with a moist ribbon of green moss running down the back. I stayed in there a long time. My feet got cramped and numb from standing in slings, but I didn't mind it at all.

When the sun got low in the sky, the heat began to relent, and I swung back to the ledge. It was cooling off, and life on the ledge was becoming enjoyable. As the sun got lower, the wall changed colors, from white to yellow, and then to orange, the color I had seen from Cathedral Peak. Now I was in the middle of that wall, where I wanted to be. Below me the cirque was filled with golden light and blue shadows. The hammering of the bong-bongs echoed off the walls, back and forth, like church bells.

Then the hammering stopped, and I started getting ready to move up. But Herb shouted down: "There's only room for one-and-a-half guys up here. You better stay there for the night."

"Crap!" I thought.

"We'll haul up our bivy gear. Put in some food and water."

"Right," I chuckled. "Enjoy that cheese. Try not to barf when you see it!"

Now it was getting dark and very cold, much colder than Yosemite Valley. Back then, the only obtainable down jackets were made by Eddie Bauer, and they were very expensive. But army down sleeping bags from war surplus stores cost much less, so that's what we had.

I pulled out my sleeping bag and wiggled into it. The puffy bag, with its smooth nylon surface, made me slide off the ledge much more quickly than before. Aid slings didn't work because the loops weren't big enough for something the size of an elephant's foot. I improvised a bigger loop, but it kept slipping off.

The only solution was to lie down on the ledge and wrap myself up in half a dozen slings and loops of rope, distributed from head to foot. These were clipped into the fixed rope above. After a lot of wriggling I managed to get all of me into the mummy bag and zipped it up. Now I was warm, but sleep was impossible. I kept sliding off the ledge, and the slings cut off circulation. Various parts of my body went to sleep that night, but I never did.

After a frosty night I rejoined my companions. The first day had been tough, but now the wall seemed more friendly. The climbing was excellent, up steep cracks and massive slabs, with rope traverses to connect the crack systems. Late in the day we reached a ledge a few hundred feet below the summit and decided to spend the night there. We might have been able to reach the top by dark—but maybe not. Climbing unknown terrain at night, with only one flashlight between us, didn't seem worth the risk. A loose block might be waiting for us, ready to crash down. And there was no need to rush it. The weather was set fair.

We settled in on the ledge. Warren took a drink from a Shmoo, made a face, and spat it out.

"Damn these Shmoos!" he said. "They're poisoning our water."

"The man at the store swore they'd never been used," I said.

"Then it must be from auto-excretion," Herb observed wryly.

The cheese was still disgusting, but the chocolate had frozen during the night, and I had wrapped it in my sleeping bag for insulation. It was still firm but hard to swallow without water.

Warren and Herb shared a can of cold pork and beans. I opened a can of sardines. They lay in neat rows in a puddle of fish oil. I took a sip. Compared to the Shmoo water, it was delicious. After I drank all the oil, those slimy little fish bodies slipped right down.

Now I felt better and could enjoy the view from our eyrie. All the peaks, from Mount Lyell to the Clark Range, Cathedral Peak, and Half Dome, were bathed in warm evening light. Lakes glittered in the last rays of the sun—they looked small enough to swallow in one gulp. In the distance headlights gleamed on the road between Tenaya Lake and Tuolumne Meadows. I could see two campfires at Budd Lake and, much closer, one at Young Lakes. Warren flashed a signal, and a small light winked back at us. Tomorrow we would be there.

The ledge was just big enough for us to sit on. Once again I spent the night trying not to fall off.

✦ ✦ ✦

We got a slow start after another wretched night, but the climbing got easier. By midday we were sitting on the summit, with knees sticking out of our pants, white T-shirts crisscrossed with dirty stripes from the hardware slings, and smelly socks peeking out from the toes of our shoes. Bits of gear were trying to escape from rips in the hauling bags, but that didn't matter now. We just sat there and grinned at each other, not saying much because our throats were so parched.

After pouring out the last of that vile Shmoo water, we scrambled down the summit ridge, looking down into the dirty-lipped, open-mouthed bergschrund of the Conness Glacier. Then it was easy going, and all the pressure of the past several days melted away.

We took long, sliding strides down the scree slopes, feeling loose and easy, making goofy attempts at yodeling like Swiss mountaineers. But in our ragged clothes, with ropes and duffel bags over our shoulders, we looked more like sailors heading for port.

And we found it at Young Lakes: feminine warmth, wine, campfire, hot food, more wine. . . .

It was the best night of my young life. A sleeping bag on flat ground. A whole lake of water to drink. And I couldn't fall off.

Steve Roper (left) and Eric Beck

7
Early Season

T he sun had just gone down on Sentinel Rock as I walked across the upper slopes of Camp 4. It was early spring, and remnants of dirty snow lingered under the trees.

I stopped at Eric Beck's camp to talk about a climb we might do. He wasn't there, but I expected him soon and, while waiting, I looked at the new home he had made for himself in Camp 4.

At one end of his table were a Primus stove, a few pots and pans, and a jug of water. The other end had a candle stuck in a wine bottle and a dozen books, with rocks as bookends. Overhead, a pack dangled from a tree limb, keeping his food safe from bears and smaller beasts.

His tent was a sheet of plastic draped over a cord stretched between two trees, with the sides held down by rocks. Holes and rips in the plastic had been patched with strips of tape. Inside, an old army down sleeping bag rested on a mattress of pine needles, with loose feathers scattered around. Next to the sleeping bag were two climbing ropes, some runners, and a sling of hardware. His climbing shoes were perched on a nearby boulder. The worn-out places glistened with a new coating of tough epoxy glue, but it didn't look like they would last through another season. They had been drying in the sun, but now the sun was long gone and it was getting very cold. I shivered when I thought about all the feathers his sleeping bag was losing.

Eric came walking up the slope, knees showing through holes in his pants. "Hey, Glen, look what I found," he said, pulling half a dozen pitons out of his pockets and tossing them on the table: two Cassin horizontals, an army ring wafer, two army angles, and a one-inch angle made by Stubai. He had spent the afternoon walking along the base of popular routes and climbing up some easy pitches in his street shoes, looking for pins the weekend climbers had dropped or failed to remove. These were standard soft iron pitons, bent out of shape from use, but hammer blows in the right places would straighten them out again. It was an impressive haul. His hardware collection was growing.

Out on the highway I heard a door slam, and a voice yelled, "Thanks for the ride," as a truck drove off. Even in the dim light there was something familiar about the figure that came walking through the woods, with a big backpack and a duffel bag over his shoulder. He paused at the end of the pavement, spotted us, and came striding up the slope with a big grin on his face.

"Roper!" Eric shouted.

"Beck! Denny! You bastards!" he chortled with glee as we shook hands. His baggage dropped to the ground, and I heard the clank of hardware inside.

"Ahhh, it's great to be back." Steve Roper's face glowed as he looked around the campground. "Nobody else here yet?"

"Nope. Just us."

"That's good. We'll get a head start. They'll never catch up with us!" He rubbed his hands together excitedly, then blew on them. "Man, it's cold. Very cold. Let's go to the Lodge. I'll set up my tent later."

We walked over to the Lodge coffee shop and waited by the cash register. The hostess walked up, a sheaf of menus riding on her hip supported by one arm.

"How many in your party?" she asked, raising her long black eyebrows.

"Three," we all said at once.

"Please come this way," she said coolly, and we followed her to one of the booths upholstered in green plastic. She was a tall platinum blonde, wearing a close-fitting knit dress and very high heels.

"Will you be having dinner?" she asked, raising her eyebrows again. We all nodded yes. Roper's mouth was ajar. She leaned over the table and placed three menus in front of us. "Do enjoy your dinner. Your waitress will be with you shortly," and she walked serenely back to the cash register.

"Who is *that*?" Roper asked, looking back over his shoulder.

"I call her the White Goddess," Beck said. "I think she's from Las Vegas."

"Is she friendly?"

"No, but very inspiring."

Our waitress came up and I ordered the usual—a #24 and a green salad.

The #24 was like a hamburger but much less expensive because the meat in it was a short, split hot dog. It cost 35 cents and was a climber's staple at the Lodge. It was the cheapest warm food you could buy. The green salad cost 35 cents, too, and came with crackers. Roper ordered the same.

"Could I just have a pot of hot water?" Beck asked.

The waitress gave him a skeptical look, picked up the menus, and left without replying.

"That's pushing it," Roper said.

"I know. But both of you ordered plenty, so it will be all right. They can't charge you for just water."

Roper and Beck hadn't seen each other all winter, so they had a lot to talk about.

"How was Mardi Gras?" Beck asked.

Roper raised his eyebrows and rolled his eyes. "You're too young for such things, Beck."

The White Goddess swept past, leading a family with young children to the booth next to us. Her scent curled in eddies into our booth.

Roper stared straight ahead but rolled his eyes again. "You shouldn't come here, Beck. This place is bad for you."

"Tell me about Mardi Gras." Beck looked down at the table, blushing in anticipation of the lurid details to come.

"Not here. Too many ears. I'll tell you later, back in camp."

The food arrived and the talking stopped. The bun of the #24 was warmly toasted. Inside, the fried wiener, onion, tomato, lettuce, and thousand island dressing made a satisfying combination. The cold weather had given me an appetite.

Beck poured some hot water into his cup from the teapot. He put some ketchup into the cup and stirred it with a spoon, adding salt and pepper and other condiments.

"Roper, are you going to eat your crackers?" he asked. Roper was chewing and shook his head no. Beck crumbled the crackers into his soup and drank it quickly, before the waitress came by again. Then he repeated the performance with my crackers.

"Ask her for more crackers, Roper."

"Beck, are you that poor? Didn't you work during the winter?"

"Yes, but it's got to last a long time."

Eric was engaged in a long-term struggle with the Curry Company to see how long he could stay in the Valley on how little money. Each time he had to part with a coin, it was a small defeat. Any day that saw the expenditure of a whole dollar was a disaster, either a failure of strategic planning and tactical daring, or a breakdown in discipline—a confession of weakness.

"You're too thin, Beck," Roper said. "You won't be strong enough for the big climbs."

"I'll be all right. It isn't really necessary to eat a lot." He paused, eying Roper's plate again. "Are you going to eat your pickle?"

Roper and I had coffee. Beck wiped his cup clean with a napkin, removing the evidence, and asked for a second pot of hot water. When it arrived, he pulled a used teabag out of his pocket and slipped it into the pot.

Roper sat back and relaxed. His hitchhike from Berkeley had taken all day, but now he was in the Valley. For the duration.

"So, just the three of us so far," he said. "No other denizens."

"That's right," I said. "But where's Pratt? I thought he would come up with you."

"It's bad news about Pratt. Brace yourselves," Roper said, pausing dramatically. He gave us a solemn look. "Pratt's in the army."

He looked at us closely, observing the impact of his announcement.

I was shocked. Chuck Pratt had lived in Camp 4 longer than anyone. It was his real home. It didn't seem possible that anything as ordinary, as banal, as the draft could ever touch him.

"They got him," Roper continued. "No Pratt in Camp 4 this year—or next year."

Beck hunched over the table on his elbows and looked quite downcast. "It's the end of an era," he said. "Where did they send him?"

"Some fort in Oklahoma."

Beck's mouth fell open. He shuddered at the thought of such utter, useless exile. Pratt might as well be in prison. Then he said, "Oh, well, at least he can write the Valley guide there. No distractions."

Beck smiled at this small victory. He unfolded the paper, laid it on the table, and pushed it forward, shyly offering it like a confession.

Roper grabbed it and scanned it hungrily. "Hmmm . . . ," he said, running his finger down the list like a gourmand examining a menu. "You begin with the short routes . . . base of El Cap, Arches Terrace, Improbable Traverse . . . cracks, face climbing, friction . . . good variety . . ."

Beck leaned over, looking proudly at the list he knew so well. The sequence had been worked out very carefully.

"Then North Dome, Bridalveil East, Arrowhead Arête—classic Powell routes. What an eye he had. Have you done Arrowhead Arête? No? It's scary but wonderful. You'll never forget your first time on it."

Beck grinned in anticipation.

"Now, the long Grade IVs: YPB, El Cap East Buttress . . ."[1] Roper went on down the list. "Worst Error! You'll die there—it'll swallow you up!"

Beck squirmed a little but retained a thin smile. This year he was going to be very bold.

"West Face of Sentinel!" Roper recoiled in mock horror. "Beck, you're not ready for that!"

"I will be, after those other climbs on the list."

In just a couple of years the West Face of Sentinel had become one of the new classics, a beautiful, clean Grade VI wall with many formidable free and aid pitches, and very few ledges.

Roper handed back the list. "So, you want to do a big wall. Are you sure you want to do *that* one?"

"I'll work up to it," Beck said, wiping his palms on his pants again. "It's very fine. I want it to be my first Grade VI."

"Then you need to do more nailing. There isn't much aid climbing on your list. All the big walls have lots of nailing. You have to practice or you'll never get up—you'll be too slow."

"Nailing is boring. All that hammering is a drag."

"You've got to do big walls if you want to be a big climber."

"I don't want to be a big climber, Roper. I want to be a *good* climber."

"Well . . . all right. But what about the West Face of Sentinel?"

"I just want to do it, and maybe Half Dome. That's all. I don't want to hammer my way up a lot of walls."

"Doing big walls is good for you. It's a matter of character."

"No, it's a matter of hammering."

"You're afraid, Beck. Admit it. Think about it: way up there, day after day, a little dot on a wall, no food or water left—you might flame out!"

"Big walls are boring. All that pounding. The greatest art is free-climbing. Hard free-climbing. It doesn't matter how big the climb is."

"No, Beck. The greatest art lies in climbing the greatest wall. You can't be satisfied with little climbs, even if they are hard. You need scale." Roper spread his arms wide. "Magnitude. You can do a 5.9 crack close to the ground, all right, but what about doing one after five days on the Salathé Wall, when you get up to that final 5.9 pitch?"

Beck fidgeted with his teaspoon. Roper seemed to have a point.

The waitress gave us a second refill and left the check on the table. That meant no more refills.

"Big walls aren't everything, Roper."

"Perhaps, but if you're going to do Sentinel West, you've got to do more nailing. Look at Denny's new route on El Cap Tree: hard aid, belays in slings, and hard free-climbing cracks, too. It's ideal preparation. Even the regular route on the Tree would be good for you. You should do it."

"The regular route is a shit route."

"Beck!" Roper said, feigning shock. "It's one of the classics! It's historic." He turned to me for support. "Denny, you like it."

"Sure," I said. "It's the first time any route ever touched the face of El Cap. It's very bold. Look at the photo in the guidebook." I was thinking of Bob Swift's photograph of the first pitch. It always had a strong effect on me.

"There, you see?" Roper said. "You should do it. It will improve your sense of Valley history. And make you respect your elders," he added.

"No. Nobody cares about those old routes anymore. It's a shit climb."

"Hah! And what about The Trowel? What would you call that?"

Beck paused, stroked his beard, and glanced up at the ceiling for inspiration. "It's a classic," he declared—struggling to keep a straight face. He had done the first ascent.

Roper burst out laughing and banged the table with his hand, making the silverware rattle. "A shit climb if there ever was one! It's a boulder sitting on a ledge. That route is ninety percent approach."

"No, Roper. It's a true classic." Beck looked down into his teacup, suppressing a giggle. "It has a certain . . . noble isolation."

We roared with laughter at the absurd claim. The White Goddess gave us a severe look from the cash register.

"Where's your list, Roper?" Beck asked, taking the offensive. "Let me see *your* list."

"I don't have one."

"Sure you do."

"I don't make lists. I don't need to. It's all in here," he said, leaning forward and tapping his temple with his forefinger, trying to look wise—without laughing.

"You've got a list, Roper. What's the matter? Afraid somebody will see it? Afraid you can't live up to it?"

"You're the one who's afraid. You haven't done one big wall yet."

"Well, I haven't failed on any, either. How many walls have you backed off of?"

By now there was a line of people at the cash register, waiting for tables. The White Goddess walked by and gave us another stern look. We didn't want to risk her disfavor so early in the season, so we drank the last of the coffee. Beck retrieved his teabag from the pot, wrapped it in a fresh napkin, and put it back in his pocket.

We paid the bill and walked back toward Camp 4 in the frosty starlight.

"Do you think the Royal Sparrow has a list?" Beck asked.

"Yeah," said Roper. "Where is Royal? What's he up to?"

Lower Yosemite Fall

8

The Ledge

I had just finished a lead and was belaying on a thin ledge three hundred feet above the ground. It was a stimulating perch because Lower Yosemite Fall was rushing past a short distance away. It plummeted down and disappeared into a cloud of mist, crashing onto the rocks below, and a deep, booming sound echoed back up the wall.

The ledge was as wide as my shoe, and I stood there facing the waterfall, with the toe of my right foot touching the heel of my left. My partner was out of sight, beneath an overhang. We couldn't hear each other because of the roar of the water. I pulled the rope up rapidly, and when it came tight I gave it some extra tugs, letting him know it was time to start climbing.

As I stood there, my eyes started following the ledge as it traversed the wall toward the waterfall. It got narrower as it went, becoming thinner and thinner, and ended about forty feet away. After that, a series of isolated footholds continued across the wall, diminishing in size until they disappeared before reaching the waterfall.

I couldn't help wondering how far I could traverse the ledge before falling off. I pictured myself out there, edging along, sweating it, getting shaky, and wishing my palms worked like suction cups. Eventually I would reach the point where, if I made one more move, I must fall.

Such thoughts were not disturbing because there was no need to actually attempt it. Instead, I looked up at the continuation of our route. The top was only a rope length away; then we would scramble along the terrace, climb down, and walk back to Camp 4.

But soon my gaze returned to the ledge. Once again I traversed it with my eyes to the end—and hesitated. Then, on a wild impulse, my vision leaped across to the waterfall. Instantly it was swept down by the power of the fall, and involuntarily I grabbed for my anchor piton.

It was exhilarating. Once again I made the crossing and leaped into the waterfall for the visual experience no physical body could survive.

Then my eyes started climbing back up the fall, struggling against the impression of increased water velocity. But when I let my vision drop back down, the opposite effect occurred. If I focused on one fragment of water and followed it down, it seemed to fall in slow motion.

Individual jets and plumes of water drifted down, swaying gracefully back and forth, forming and dissolving before disappearing into the mist. I saw many shades of blue, green, and white I had never noticed before. Beams of sunlight and shadow flickered and pulsed through the column of water. It was mesmerizing, and I began to lose sense of time and place.

Suddenly I felt a light tap on my foot. I looked down and saw a small green frog sitting on my shoe. He had jumped out of a crack and landed on my foot. He looked around for a while and then hopped down onto the ledge. It was a strange place to meet an animal. I kept quite still, wondering what he would do next.

He looked around some more and then began hopping along the ledge, taking shorter jumps as it narrowed down to an inch, for his body was about that wide. As the ledge became even thinner, he stopped hopping and started crawling, very slowly. His body tilted over the edge as he inched along, with two feet pressing against the wall on one side and the long toes of his other feet clutching the outside edge. After several starts and stops he reached the end of the ledge.

To my surprise he didn't try to turn around. Instead, he was looking ahead to the first isolated foothold. It was small and rounded. I could see him shift his feet and hunch his back in preparation. Then he leaped for the hold and grabbed it with his front feet, quickly scrabbling his hind feet up and getting them onto his new perch.

I looked ahead for the next hold. It was smaller than the first one, and I thought surely he would turn back. But he kept going, made his next leap, and this time barely managed to hold on.

The palms of my hands were sweating as I watched him struggling for balance on the new hold. His body was much too wide for it and kept tipping outward. There wasn't room enough for his feet, and he kept shifting them, one atop the other. He clung to the hold for about a minute, and then I could see that he was going to leap again, to an even tinier hold.

At last he made his leap. Perhaps the awkward position and poor footing threw his aim a little off. Perhaps the next hold was just too small. He clutched it briefly with his front feet, but the momentum of his body was too great and it pulled him off. Without a sound he fell down the wall, turning over and over, and disappeared into the mist.

Slogging through the snow

9
Bad Weather

I could see why he needed to get to the Valley so badly.

I rummaged through my daypack and pulled out *Riprap and Cold Mountain Poems*, by Gary Snyder. This was a good time for it, I thought. As I read, I started hearing things more acutely. The rain made a steady tapping on the tarp, with splats and plops from big drops falling from the tree branches. Gary set cooking pots out in the rain to collect water. The raindrops pinged and ponged into them, then the tones changed to plinks and plunks as the pots filled.

To the east, Yosemite Falls was booming. Across the Valley, to the south, Sentinel Falls added a lighter tone. To the north, a new waterfall fed by the storm was coming down the wall behind Camp 4. It was a fine triphonic concert.

Raindrops glistened on the edges of the tarp and tent. Up close, the colors were sharp and vivid. The carpets of oak leaves and pine needles on the ground were a rich golden brown. The patches of moss on the boulders were usually dark and dusty, but now the rain had made them a bright yellow-green.

Farther away, everything was soft and misty. Fragments of the Valley walls came and went in the clouds. The storm had laid a heavy gray lid on the rim and was pushing it down, lower and lower, as it got colder.

As I looked around, a slight motion in the bushes at the end of Camp 4 caught my eye. A coyote's head appeared, his eyes staring straight at me. He drew back, but after a minute his head reappeared. I nudged Gary, and we both watched as he emerged from the brush and trotted down the slope.

"Making his rounds," Gary said.

The coyote sniffed around some campsites and garbage cans and kept glancing at us in a nervous way. Perhaps he had migrated to Yosemite from the flatlands, where it was always open season on coyotes. He crossed the highway, heading for the meadow.

"He'll be hunting mice and ground squirrels," Gary said.

A minute later a bear emerged from the same bushes and sauntered down the slope. He wasn't nervous. This was *his* campground. He snuffled around the garbage cans but found nothing. It would be slim pickings until the tourists arrived. Then he followed the coyote across the highway. Perhaps he could scare him off a kill.

I wanted to climb, but everything was drenched in cold water. Then I thought of El Capitan Tree. The first pitch went up under a big roof, using a bolt ladder on the left. But some thin cracks led directly up to the roof and then out left, above the bolts. Bypassing the bolt ladder would be an excellent challenge and, under the roof, it should be dry. If it was still raining tomorrow, I wanted to try it.

Gary knew the route well. The Tree stood on a grassy ledge four hundred feet above the talus, under another big roof. Water dropped from the roof onto the ledges for most of the year, sustaining a population of plants and small animals. For one of his biology projects, Gary had done a study to discover which of these life forms had crept up the wall, floated in on the air, or oozed down the wall to this special place.

I had my own history with the Tree. The first pitch was spectacular and photogenic. So was its rappel, which dropped down over the roof and left you far from the wall, spinning slowly in the air. The first time I went down it, the ropes slipped off my shoulder pad and started cutting into my shoulder.[1] It was a hot day, and I was wearing only a T-shirt. I wasn't far from the ground, so I gritted my teeth and kept on going. I could hear the rope ends rustling in a patch of dry grass on the ground below, but there was something odd about the sound. I looked down and saw a rattlesnake. The ropes had made him angry, and his tail was buzzing.

The pain in my shoulder was terrible, but a snakebite would be worse. I shook the rope ends, thrashing them back and forth in the grass. Perhaps the snake thought he was facing a superior creature. He slunk away, and I was able to land and end the pain. After that, I had two parallel scars on my shoulder. I had joined a special club. People who climbed the Tree liked to tug on the necks of their shirts and show off their rappel scars.

It was getting dark in Camp 4 and I was hungry. I went to the car and returned with a can of pork and beans, but Gary suggested something better. He lowered his food bag from a tree limb, and in a few minutes he was frying up a pan of sliced onions, mushrooms, and tomatoes. He cracked some eggs and tossed them in, along with some diced cheese. A few flips with the spatula, and there it was—the perfect antidote to a cold, wet day. We ate directly out of the pan. No need to make more dirty dishes.

As we ate, Gary told me about the Boojum tree, which was named after an imaginary creature invented by Lewis Carroll. In 1922, a biologist was in Sonora, Mexico, collecting plant specimens for the University of Arizona. One afternoon he focused his telescope on a hillside of strange-looking plants shaped like spiny, upside-down carrots. Some of them were fifty feet tall. On the spur of the moment, he said, "Ho, ho! A Boojum. Definitely a Boojum!" The name stuck. Biology didn't have to be serious all the time.

After dinner the rain was still coming down, and I knew it would be warm and mellow around the fireplace in the lounge at Yosemite Lodge. But it was too easy to spend money there. We lit some candles and read more books until we got sleepy.

Back in the tent I listened to the rain. Apparently it would go on forever. But in the middle of the night it stopped, and I went to sleep with visions of sunshine, blue skies, and steam rising from the walls as they dried out. A few hours later I felt the tent pressing in on me. I pushed back, heard a plop, and the tent sprang back into shape. I turned on the flashlight, unzipped the entrance, and looked out. It was snowing!

In the morning, I trudged through a foot of fresh snow to Gary's camp. He wasn't there, and I could see his tracks going down the slope. The snowfall was heavy but silent. The only sounds were dull thumps when overloaded tree branches shed their burdens of snow and then sprang back up.

I didn't want another day at the table, this time in a down jacket, balaclava, legs in a sleeping bag, trying to read a book while wearing mittens. I walked down the slope to the campground road and headed for the Lodge. On the right, most of the tables on the flat ground were unoccupied. The thick snow made them look like giant white layer cakes, floating off the ground in the dark woods. On the left, lines of tracks came down the slope from the climbers' camps, all heading for the Lodge. Someone's initials were drawn in the snow. They had a yellow color.

The highway was freshly plowed, but the snow was piling up fast. Where was all this frozen stuff coming from? It was supposed to be spring!

✦ ✦ ✦

I kicked the snow off my boots, pulled open the double doors of the lounge, and entered a world of warmth. It was a very large room, with sofas, chairs, and tables arranged in comfortable groups. The walls were huge plate-glass windows, from floor to ceiling, giving panoramic views of the Valley, especially Yosemite Falls.

Near one end, in the center of the room, was a round fireplace. Its chimney was supported by brick pillars. Fallen trees had been sawed and hewn into fragrant wedges of cedar, oak, and ponderosa for firewood. As they glowed on the grate, their warmth and aromas made the storm go away.

My friends were reading by the fire. I pulled up a chair next to Roper. He was reading *Lolita*, and a smile kept playing over his lips. On the other side of the fire, Frank Sacherer was reading *The Complete Sherlock Holmes*. It was a very thick volume that might last as long as the storm. Bill Amborn was sitting next to him, reading Thucydides. He had dropped out of UC Berkeley, and now that he didn't have to read it he was enjoying it.

Beck was writing in his diary. He would stare at the fire with a blank expression on his face. Then suddenly he would smile and scribble another entry. It made you wonder what he was thinking.

Colliver was reading *Die Drei Letzten Probleme der Alpen*—The Last Three Problems of the Alps—by Anderl Heckmair. One of the photos in it showed two climbers relaxing on a ledge in the middle of a steep wall. They were smiling, singing, and one was playing a harmonica. Gary translated the caption for me: "Thus appeared the death candidates." They were killed on a climb a short time later.

I opened my daypack and pulled out *Lonely Challenge*, by Hermann Buhl. There he was, with the withered old-man's face Nanga Parbat had given him. He died a few years later, pushing the limits on a peak in the Karakoram. He was at the top of his game, doing what he loved best. Perhaps he could have lived to eighty, hobbling around with a cane, but that didn't seem like the right end for someone like him.

Royal and Liz Robbins came in the door and took off their French-made down jackets. Despite the bad weather, they were looking quite stylish. Both were wearing white, long-sleeved turtleneck T-shirts, tan corduroy knickers, and white knee socks. Royal sat down on a couch, got out his binder, and started writing his next article for a climbing journal. He placed a dictionary on one side and a thesaurus on the other. Liz curled up nearby with a novel.

I leafed through a collection of short stories and selected "To Build a Fire," by Jack London. Roper glanced over and saw what I was reading.

"That's a good one," he chuckled.

Yes, I thought, every climber should read it.

The hours passed, and the snow kept falling. The Valley had disappeared. There was nothing to look at, and the lounge began to fill up. The polished floors were wet from the melted snow that got tracked in, and the carpets were getting muddy. An old janitor was busy with a mop and vacuum cleaner, trying to maintain order. The tourists had no place else to go. The cafeteria was closed between lunch and dinner, the coffee shop had a long line, and the bar wasn't open yet. One of the tourists asked, "Where's the bowling alley?" "Fresno," Beck replied.

There was a buzz of chatter, and children were running around out of control, but suddenly we heard a new sound—faint but distinct. The tourists didn't hear it, but the climbers snapped to attention. Rock fall! We jumped up and rushed outside. Where was it? We listened intently, but it was over, and the echoes faded away. When the snow melted, we would scan the walls closely, looking for fresh white rock scars.

I went into the gift shop and bought a PayDay for lunch. It was the biggest candy bar you could get for a dime. Coated with nuts instead of chocolate and sugar, it almost seemed like real food.

Back in the lounge, everyone had resumed their places. There were some new arrivals. Harry Daley was writing a note for the *Sierra Club Bulletin* about a new route he had done. In a far corner of the room Mike Borghoff was hunched over a table, writing a poem. Normally a loquacious fellow, he didn't want to talk to anyone right now.

As the afternoon wore on, Royal and Liz left to have high tea at The Ahwahnee. The rest of us tried to make the time pass in various ways: Chess. Cards. Crossword puzzles. Board games. Rock, paper, scissors. Thumb wrestling. Arm wrestling.

Gary was playing a subtler game—haiku. He sat by a window with a notepad on his knee, staring out at the falling snow, occasionally writing brief phrases.

"What's he doing?" someone asked me. "Counting snowflakes?"

"No. Syllables, I think."

Suddenly Roper walked back in and announced, "The bar is open. I'll buy the beer." Six of us went in, sat down, and a friendly waiter came over. He climbed a little.

"We'll have one beer and six bowls of popcorn!" Roper ordered in a grand manner. The popcorn was free. It was cold and stale, but it could ease your hunger. The Ansel Adams photographs on the walls were much more satisfying. I walked around the room, looking at them closely, engraving their perfections on my visual memory.

The bartender was named Ade. He was big and burly, and nobody messed with him. He could see that we were exploiting the system a little, but that was OK as long as we didn't overdo it and didn't get too boisterous.

There was an interesting story about Ade. Late one night a rowdy guest was getting drunk and started cursing the park rangers in a loud voice because he had gotten a speeding ticket. Ade came over and asked him to please quiet down.

Someone at the table said the ranger was right. This enraged the rowdy. He yelled and threw his glass at the man. Ade quickly returned, put his left arm around the rowdy's shoulder, and delivered a short tap on the jaw with his right. He levered him up, and they started walking out of the room arm in arm. "That's all right," Ade reassured his customers. "It's all right now." Nobody noticed that the rowdy was unconscious and his feet were dragging on the floor.

Beck left for a minute and then came back with a big grin on his face. "It's bones night!" he said, with a gleam in his eye. Leaving our friends to their popcorn, Beck, Roper, and I headed toward the cafeteria.

On the way, Roper stopped at a pay phone and called a friend in Berkeley. "Yeah, no point in coming up, unless you bring an ice ax and crampons. The road might be closed."

As he talked, I watched tourists feeding a raccoon. It was sitting up in a cute pose they couldn't resist. They gave it some candy and walked on. The coons in Camp 4 weren't so polite. They were aggressive opportunists. Roper hung up and looked down at the coon.

"Scram!" he said, and stomped his foot. The coon growled back, his fur bristled, and he didn't move.

"Truculent little bastard, aren't you," Roper said.

We reached the cafeteria and stood in line. It wouldn't open for a while, but you didn't want to miss out on bones. Once in a while the cafeteria served prime rib. The chefs sliced it off racks of ribs. The ribs still had small bits of high-quality beef attached here and there. Instead of throwing them in the garbage, the Curry Company had discovered that they could sell a plateful of these bones to certain characters for fifty cents. We were always first in line.

When the cafeteria opened, we didn't go through the regular food line like everyone else. We went directly to the cashier at the far end of the line, said "bones," and paid her fifty cents each. While we waited, I noticed some mischievous Boy Scouts switching the contents of sugar and salt shakers. We suffered attacks of salivation as the tourists carried their plates of prime rib past us. At last, enough of it had been sold, and plates of bones were handed to us.

We carried our gustatory trophies to a table and ate in silence, gnawing on the bones like wolves in a story about the Yukon. Then we sat back and burped in satisfaction. I noticed that Beck's bones were cleaner than everyone else's.

The meat was worth the money, but actually, at the cafeteria, you didn't have to pay anything. There was lots of free food on the tables if you were bold enough to claim it. In their package deals at the Lodge the tourists were entitled to more food than they could eat, and when they left the table, some of it would be untouched. There were cubes of brightly colored Jell-O, with slices of peach and pear suspended inside. The crisp sesame-sprinkled rolls were excellent and came with butter and jam.

You had to be desperate if you wanted to try the cold, glazed-over chicken à la king or the mashed potatoes with congealed gravy. But there might be a half-eaten slice of roast beef. You could cut into it from the untouched side, leaving a thin strip of meat in the middle, a kind of "cordon sanitaire." And sometimes for dessert there would be a wedge of apple pie sitting in a puddle of melted vanilla ice cream.

A late arrival joined us. The bones were all gone by now, but he was very hungry. A family of tourists had just gotten up from the table next to us, and there were tempting things on it. Kids often refused to eat food that looked different from what they were used to getting at home.

He kept glancing over at the table.

"No. Don't," Roper said. "You'll get us in trouble."

"But it's still warm! If the busboy gets it, it'll just go in the garbage."

"Don't do it. The manager is looking at us. It's time to go."

We got up and walked toward the door, but our famished friend stayed behind. As we left, I could hear a clatter of dishes. The conveyor belt carrying the trays of dirty dishes had jammed up, and they were crashing to the floor.

Back in the lounge, it was time for the movie. Over the years, a number of half-hour travelogues about Yosemite had been made, and each night one of them was shown. Tonight it would be the best of them, *Valley of Light.* Roper and I had seen it many times and had memorized its more portentous lines. We stood in back, where we couldn't be heard, and took turns reciting them just before they were spoken on-screen.

It began with a sequence about Ansel Adams. I led off with, "I have pointed my camera ten thousand times at the rocks and water that surround my home. . . ." A few minutes later, Roper solemnly intoned, "A few miles to the south stands our living link with the past, the giant sequoias." I came back with, "Few people see, or even *know* about, the *High* Country."

After the lights came back on, Roper and I continued with other games. One of them was identifying quotes from climbing literature. He started off with, "Maurice—your hands!"

"That's from *Annapurna.*" I pondered a bit and then said, "Two nightmarish walls spun away into the sky, forming an immense open book."

Roper tilted his chair back and gazed at the ceiling. "Aha, I've got it. *The West Face*, by Magnone." He stared into the fire, scratching his chin, and then said, "The last orange peel escaped, went spinning down the slope, and danced across the snow."

"That's a fine one. It's by Steck—'Yosemite Point Buttress.'"

After a dozen more quotes, we went on to another game—identifying climbs after hearing part of the route description. Roper began with, "This pinnacle is not a pinnacle. It's a ledge partway up a wall. Starting from a bay tree, pendulum left to a . . ."

"Rixon's Pinnacle." He was annoyed that I got it so fast. Now it was my turn. "The first pitch is an easy-looking low-angle chimney, but the rock is polished and slippery. There's a chockstone at the top."

Roper was ready to pounce.

"Above the chimney, climb a series of steps, leading up and right . . ."

"The Arches!" he exclaimed gleefully. He knew all the classic routes by heart. "How about this one? The first pitch is 5.9, up steep cracks. The second pitch is slightly easier—5.8—but it's a completely unprotected chimney a hundred and fifty feet long."

"Is the last pitch a 5.10 shallow, overhanging jam crack?" I asked.

"Yes."

"There's only one climb like that, thank God. It's the Crack of Doom."

Our final game was visual identification. We went to the gift shop, where they had coffee-table books of Yosemite landscapes. With sheets of blank paper, one of us would cover most of a photograph, leaving only part of a crack system or a ledge visible, and challenge the other to name the wall.

Back in the lounge, the fire was nearly out. Lodge employees started turning out the lights and locking the doors. It was time for the night crew to clean up the day's mess and wax the floors.

Roper and I put on sweaters and anoraks and walked back to Camp 4, following the trench made by the denizens. The snow was up to our knees, and it was still coming down.

Monday Morning Slab in Winter

10
The Icy Game

We headed out toward Monday Morning Slab. The road was plowed only as far as Camp Curry. We parked and trudged up the road, taking turns breaking trail. Turning right, we came to a clearing in the forest. A white cone rose up in the middle of it, looking like a miniature Aleutian volcano. Despite all the snow, a thin wisp of smoke was rising from its summit. This was the Valley garbage dump, a favorite hangout for the bears. Usually there would be a bunch of them scrounging around, digging into the pile and fighting over the choice bits, but today there were none. Perhaps they were thinking about going back into hibernation.

We wallowed uphill through the deep snowdrifts and arrived at the base of Glacier Point Apron, a smooth slab almost two thousand feet high. Although its angle was only 50 degrees, it had been highly polished by the glaciers. Its first ascent had called for the most delicate, continuous friction climbing in Yosemite, on tiny holds that were barely visible. Now they were buried under snow and ice, and such climbing was clearly impossible.

The Apron's only weakness was Monday Morning Slab. This was a triangular exfoliation slab, four hundred feet high. Its right edge, where it joined the Apron, consisted of easy cracks. It was a popular beginner's climb, rated 5.1, and we were used to scampering up and down it unroped, wearing only shoes and shorts. Now it was quite transformed.

The snow on the slab was too soft to climb on—it just slipped off if you put any weight on it. Under the snow, the rock was glazed with a thin veneer of ice that flaked off when pricked by ax or crampons. But thicker ribbons of ice had formed in the corners where the exfoliation layers overlapped each other, providing enough ice to climb. If the first climbers up a pitch shattered the ice, the last ones jammed their ax and crampon points directly into the cracks and struggled up.

It was a slippery game. Many pitons were used for protection. In one place, where the holds could not be found—we knew they were down there somewhere under all that frosting—we used a piton for direct aid.

Handling the hardware called for removing our mittens, and the numbness came quickly. I had to look at my fingers to make sure they were obeying orders. At the next belay ledge, I would stick them down in my crotch, under the clothes, and be happy when I felt the excruciating, burning sensation in my fingers. It meant the blood was coming back, and circulation would be restored.

Our route ended on a small ledge at the top of the slab, and we watched avalanches hissing down the Apron. They had been falling the whole time, but our pointed slab had divided them and saved us from destruction.

I stood there looking up into the white void. A featureless sheet of snow went on in all directions and disappeared into the mists. Suddenly the whole surface avalanched, and everything was sliding down except me. Then the impression reversed itself, and it seemed like the snow was motionless, and I was gliding up the Apron on the prow of a ship.

Frank Sacherer

11
One Inch

The North Buttress of Lower Cathedral Rock begins with a Gothic arch two hundred feet high. Two cracks shoot up the wall, curve in, and meet under a roof.

I led up the left-hand crack. It was mixed free and aid, and I belayed at a small ledge. Sacherer nailed up the second pitch and belayed in slings under the roof. The cracks that led over the roof were poor and loose. Piton placement was marginal, but I wasn't worried. If I fell from the roof, I would stop in midair and not crash into anything.

Above the roof, a single crack continued up the vertical wall, and I was nearly out of pitons by the time I came to a tiny ledge just big enough for two feet. I anchored in and called down to Frank that I was ready to haul.

The first ascent of this route had taken two days. It had been climbed twice since then, each ascent taking one very long day. We would have done the same except that I wanted to do a major variation. The bivouac ledge used on the first ascent was several hundred feet above me. From there, the route diagonaled up and right to the crest. But I wanted to do a direct finish. A very steep, smooth wall rose directly above the bivy ledge, looking more formidable than anything else on the buttress. It would take many hours to climb it, and that was why we had the hauling bag. We hoped to get partway up the wall, descend to the bivy ledge for the night, and finish the climb the next day. The direct wall had a good crack system, but some of the cracks looked wide so a big selection of bong-bongs was in the bag, along with food, water, and our bivouac gear.

I hauled the bag up hand over hand, anchored it in, and yelled down to Frank that he was on belay. It would take some time for him to remove all the pitons, so I could relax and look around.

The granite here was a dark slate gray. Because it faced north, it got less sun than other walls, and the rock was mottled with patches of moss and lichens.

Across the Valley, the great white wall of El Capitan gleamed in the sunlight, pure and smooth. Our route was good practice in the techniques needed to climb El Cap, but it would take many North Buttresses, stacked one on top of another, to equal that wall. Our route could be done in a day. On The Nose, it would take a week of such days.

But now, in 1962, it was beginning to seem possible. If this climb went well, Frank and I would do some bigger ones—and then we would dare to make the attempt. El Cap had been climbed three times, and we wanted to be next.

Frank reached my ledge and clipped the daypack into the anchor. We munched some gorp and looked up the wall. The aid crack continued above us, then the angle relented, the rock became more broken, and it looked like free-climbing would take us to the bivy ledge. That would go fast and give us plenty of time to make a good start on the direct finish.

Frank was halfway up the next pitch when he came to a steep, shallow corner.

"I think this might go free." He looked down at me with a grin. "I'll try it. The protection is good."

"OK, I've got you," I said. Frank always wanted to push the limits. Hard free-climbing was what he liked best.

He started up the corner, but neither liebacking nor jamming worked very well. There were no face holds, and the walls of the corner were too steep for stemming on friction. Ten feet above his last piton and growling with frustration, he was about to fall when he saw an edge of rock sticking out from behind the right side of the corner. He put his right foot on it for cross-pressure to save himself from falling. But the edge of rock was a tiny part of a big flake that was sitting on a ledge, just out of sight.

Frank shouted and I looked up. Time went into slow motion as I watched the flake tilt out from the wall, topple over, and start rumbling down the wall right at me. It must have weighed several tons.

I had to escape, but where could I go? The ledge was just two feet long, surrounded by sheer walls. I decided that my only chance was to wait until the flake got close and then jump off into space as it plummeted past. When I hit the end of the rope it would pull Frank off his holds. We would both be dangling in the air, but the rope was clipped into a number of pitons. It might work. It was my only chance.

But it couldn't work. It would take too long to undo my anchors. The rock would hit before I could jump.

I looked back up. The flake was grinding and scraping down the wall. It was coming straight at me, and I realized that in one second I would be dead. Instinctively, I put my hands over my head and tried to make myself smaller.

As I waited for it to hit I wondered what it would be like. I thought there would be an intense flash of white light and pain, then everything would go black, and that would be my last experience. After that I would be a red streak on the wall.

The rock smashed my left foot but—somehow—missed my upper body. The hauling bag, dangling against my left leg, was swept away, leaving eight clean grommets on a loop of rope. Where was it? I looked down. The bag had burst and our gear was scattered on the talus below. In my shocked state I yelled up, "Frank, we forgot the hauling bag!"

He gave me a puzzled look and said, "Can we go on now?"

That snapped it. "You bastard!" I shouted. "You nearly killed me! My foot is broken! We have to go down!"

I tried to calm down and clear my head because I would have to help with my own rescue. As he descended, Frank hammered out the pitons he had placed; they would be needed for rappel anchors. The rock fall had cut our hauling line in several places. It would be useless for rappelling, but the belay line was intact. With one rope it would take six rappels to descend three pitches.

My foot was a throbbing mass of pain and numbness. We had codeine in the first-aid kit for situations like this, but I decided not to take it. Reduced pain would allow me to move my foot more, and that could cause more damage. Inside, I could feel things moving around. Perhaps pieces of bone were cutting into tendons. To limit the damage, I decided I shouldn't move my foot at all. That meant I couldn't rappel.

As Frank lowered me down, I pushed my body away from the rock with both hands and one foot, while the other foot dangled in the air. After half a rope length, I drove in pitons and established a new anchor. Frank rappelled and pulled down the rope, and we repeated the process until, after several hours of careful work, we reached the ground.

We left the gear there, and I started hobbling down the talus on one foot, supported by Frank. But the rocks were too unstable and kept shifting as I hopped down the slope, and I nearly fell over. I couldn't afford to land on my broken foot, so the only answer was to go down on my rump. I pushed myself up with both hands and one foot, while Frank held the broken foot off the ground by grabbing the cuff of my pant leg. Progress was slow. It must have been a strange sight as we inched down the talus, pathetic and comic at the same time.

It was nearly dark by the time we reached the road and drove to the hospital near Yosemite Village. I checked in, got examined, and spent the night in a hospital bed.

The day had started so beautifully and now it was a disaster. I was staring morosely at the ceiling when I heard a tapping on the window. I parted the curtain and saw two beaming faces. They were the Johnson sisters, Reva and Kay. Frank had told them about what happened, and they had come over to cheer me up. I opened the window, and they wanted to hear all about it. They were very sympathetic. It seemed like they both wanted to hug me at the same time.

"We brought you a special treat," Reva said with a big smile.

She produced a bottle of riesling from her daypack.

Wow! Just what I needed.

I unhooked the screen and she passed it in. While I pulled the cork, she brought out three wine glasses. Kay laid a row of fancy hors d'oeuvres on the windowsill. Where had she gotten them—from The Ahwahnee? The wine was chilled, the food was delicious, and for a while I stopped feeling sorry for myself. Maybe being an invalid wouldn't be so bad.

The next day Dr. Avery Sturm and his assistant came into my room.

"Aha!" he said with a jovial smile. "Here you are at last. We've been expecting you!" He said that to all the climbers who visited him.

He anesthetized me, and they started massaging my foot, pushing the bones back into place. They were treating it like putty, but there was no pain. As they worked, they laughed and made jokes as if they were playing cards. I felt like saying, "Hey, be careful. That's a very important foot."

Afterward, they put on a cast. As I lay there, waiting for the plaster to harden, I wondered what was next. El Capitan had looked so inspiring, but there would be no El Cap this year. Would I ever get to attempt it? Would I be able to climb anything? If climbing was over, what would I do?

I knew I was lucky to be alive. If I couldn't climb, perhaps I could write about it. Climbing had given me my finest experiences, and they were alive in my head. Yesterday, death had missed me by one inch. Now I had been given the chance to keep those experiences from disappearing.

Party in Camp 4

12
Climber Central

veteran climber. Now he was bigger than Fitschen, but the nickname stuck.

Foott was the opposite of Little Joe. He was long, tall, and pensive, and so lean that when he was asleep in his sleeping bag, it looked like no one was in it. But he was very strong and had been a wrestler before he found climbing. In Yosemite, he quickly rose to a high level. He and Bill Amborn became the first all-teenaged team to climb the Steck-Salathé Route on Sentinel Rock. After that, with Little Joe and Rich Calderwood, they made the first long climbs on Glacier Point Apron, the hardest friction climbing in North America at that time. Today they were headed back to the Apron, wanting to play more of that slippery game.

The next table along the slope was occupied by Bob Kamps and Mark Powell. After spending their early years on the big walls, they were now creating shorter but intensely difficult routes, pushing free-climbing into new realms of boldness. Kamps was looking more wolfish than ever. The deep creases on his cheeks made him look too tough to be a grammar school teacher.

Powell was walking with an obvious limp. In 1957 he had been making the first ascent of the face of El Capitan with Warren Harding and Bill Feuerer, but on a day off he fell on a short, easy climb and suffered a compound fracture of his ankle that became badly infected. He nearly lost the foot. Instead, the doctors fused the ankle, and now, after years of struggle, he was once again climbing at a very high level.

Today they would be searching for another climb of exquisite mental and physical difficulty.

Sacherer and Colliver were at the next campsite, trying out some new climbing gear—automobile tire inner tubes. Frank was always trying to free-climb things that other people preferred to ignore. He had found an unusually nasty off-width crack that was scraping the skin off his knees. Kneepads seemed to be the answer, but basketball pads were too soft and mushy. Hard pads, worn by motorcycle racers and floor installers, were too stiff and skittered off the rock.

Frank cut a one-foot section of an inner tube, pulled it up over his knee, and dropped the pant leg back down. It was a snug fit and might work. A second layer would reduce the pain even more, and it could be put on over the pants. The rubber surface against the rock might increase the friction, like the rubber sole on a shoe. It was worth a try.

I wished them luck and hobbled on. Beck's camp was empty. He had left at dawn with Galen Rowell. They were attempting a multiday route that had been climbed only once.

I headed downhill, and by now the crutches were chafing my armpits. The slope of Camp 4 seemed steeper and less stable than before, and it took longer to get to the outhouse. On the way back, I ran into Roper.

"How's the foot?" he asked. "I heard about it from Sacherer."

"Not too bad. Know of any climbs for the right foot?"

Roper was talking to someone from the Iowa Mountaineers. We had always been surprised to hear that a state with no mountains could have mountaineers. This was his first visit to Yosemite, and he was asking Steve to recommend a climb.

"Well, tell me the kind of climb you'd like to do, and I'll pick one out. You know—how hard, how long? Face climbing? Or cracks: chimneys, jam cracks, liebacks? Friction? Aid climbing: easy, hard, overhanging?"

"Umm . . . Well . . ."

"Straight up, or indirect with intricate route finding? An old classic or something new? Strenuous or relaxed? Scary or safe?"

A doubtful expression came over the visitor's face. He hadn't expected it to be so complicated.

"Want it to be 5.5, 5.6, 5.7, 5.8?"

"What?"[1]

I continued up the slope and was surprised to see Beck back at his camp. They had climbed only a few pitches and then retreated. Galen was already zooming back to Berkeley in his souped-up car. He owned a car repair shop, and each time he came to the Valley, it was in a different hot rod. His business had made him, in our eyes, relatively wealthy. He had arrived with a selection of gourmet food for the bivouacs and left it all with Beck, who was now gorging himself. It was the best meal he'd had in a long time.

"So how was it?" I asked.

"It's a shit climb. A real shit climb."

"Scary?"

"Ugly. Dirty cracks stuffed with munge and loose rocks. Dead little trees behind expanding flakes. Rotten roofs hanging over your head—it looked like they had missing teeth. Ugh!" he shivered. "It's a house of cards. You really don't want to go up there."

Allen Steck and Dick Long came striding up the slope with triumphant grins on their faces. They had just climbed the Steck-Salathé on Sentinel in a day and a half. Steck had been on the five-day first ascent of that famous route long ago, in 1950, so this was a most impressive performance by him.

One of the tourists was interested in climbing. He had heard that Yvon Chouinard and TM Herbert were attempting a new route on the north face of Sentinel. He had a telescope mounted on a tripod and had been trying to find them, panning the scope up and down and from side to side, without success. Roper took a look, and in a few seconds he said, "There they are."

One by one we all peered through the scope. It was an impressive sight: two tiny dots clinging to a dark, sheer wall. Their white shirts made them easy to find but only if you knew where to look. And you couldn't be sure until one of the white dots moved. Otherwise, it might be a white flake or a water-polished chockstone.

They were doing a direct route on the smooth wall in the middle of the face, left of the Steck-Salathé. This was their second day on the face, and they were about halfway up. Jan Herbert, TM's wife, took a look.

"How are they doing?" she asked.

"They're doing fine. Making good progress," I said.

"Will they reach the summit today?" she asked anxiously.

"Hard to say. There's a barrier of roofs above them, and the wall above that looks pretty blank for a ways. It will probably require some bolts, so it will take a while."

"If they don't reach the top, will they get to a bivouac ledge?"

"I don't see any. But don't worry. They've had nights like that before."

"Oh, no! Poor TM!" She walked away with Liz Robbins, who was inviting her to have tea at The Ahwahnee.

Roper swung the scope left and looked at Yosemite Point Buttress. It was being attempted by climbers he had met in the Tetons. They had done the biggest climbs in that range, and Roper had invited them to Yosemite, rec-ommending the buttress, known as YPB, as a good test of their skills.

"No sign of them," he said. "It's afternoon, and they still haven't reached the pedestal. Those Teton climbers are so slow! They might have to biv-ouac." The route was usually done in one long day.

Back at my table, I straightened out a wire coat hanger and pushed it down inside my cast to scratch an itch on my ankle. I was eating a peanut butter sandwich when another familiar figure came walking up the slope and said, "Howdy." It was Charlie Fisher. I had met him at Modesto Junior College, where he was a counselor and psychology teacher. He was a mountaineer, and I had introduced him to Yosemite rock climbing, guiding him up the Royal Arches and the Lost Arrow Spire. That was as far as he wanted to go in the Valley. We'd had good times together and shook hands enthusiastically, but his smile faded when he saw the cast on my leg.

"How'd you get that?" he asked.

I explained what had happened.

"I'd heard that you've been moving on to bigger things, but . . . isn't this taking it too far?"

Charlie was from Texarkana, a town that straddled the border between Texas and Arkansas, and it was always a surprise to hear his mellow Southern accent on a belay ledge. He had gone to graduate school in Boulder, Colorado, where he caught the climbing bug, but he stayed rea-sonable about it. He wanted a balanced life, and climbing was only part of it. He was a "recreational" climber and proud of it.

"Yessir," he said. "After a weekend at Tuolumne Meadows, after climb-ing Cathedral Peak or Mount Lyell, when I get back to the office on Monday morning I feel 're-created.' That's what climbing is for."

Just then Royal Robbins walked up. He was carrying a sling of hardware and clunked it onto the table. I introduced him to Charlie.

"Hi," Royal said, with a quick, thin smile. "Glen, I want to do that new route you did near Lower Yosemite Fall—the Black Wall. How does this selection look?"

I pawed through it. There was a good variety of horizontals and angles, with some bong-bongs and knifeblades. "That should do it."

"Think it will go free?"

It better not, I thought to myself. At least not right away. Not on the second ascent.

"Nooo . . . probably not . . . but maybe," I said.

Royal was hot to add another scalp to his belt. I could see a long row of water bottles on his table. He was testing them for leaks. Tom Frost would arrive in a couple of days, and they would attempt something big, but Royal wouldn't say what it was. He just said, "Haven't decided yet." But he was an expert chess player, and I was sure he had his next moves all planned out.

Charlie didn't like competition in the mountains—it interfered with the enjoyment of primal nature. And competition led to increased risk. Charlie had read Royal's climbing articles, which described cutting-edge adventures at the limits of the possible.

"How do you justify taking all that risk?" Charlie asked.

"There's no *need* to justify it. It's an act of free will," Royal said brusquely. He picked up the hardware and walked back to his camp.

"Doesn't want to talk about it, does he? Interesting. . . ." Charlie looked around at Camp 4 and then at the walls rising above it. He didn't feel at home here.

"How are your parents? And your little sisters? Haven't seen them in quite a spell."

"They're fine. Still in Livingston."

"How do they feel about that?" He pointed at the cast.

"Not good. But they know it's out of their hands now."

"You won't be able to climb for a long time. Ever think about going back to school?"

"Sometimes. But there are things I have to do here first."

"Well, you take care of yourself," he said as he got up to leave. "Don't push it too far."

"I won't."

"I wish I could be sure of that. Remember, climbing isn't everything."

But in those years, it was.

✦ ✦ ✦

It was late afternoon now, and the light on Sentinel was changing. In the morning, it had been a dark, looming monolith that presented a challenge with no obvious solutions. During the day, it had lightened up, turned various shades of blue and gray, and began revealing its secrets. The north face slanted slightly to the west, and in the afternoon the sun started raking across the wall, throwing highlights and shadows, revealing crack systems and ledges that had been invisible before.

From my table I studied the wall through binoculars. I found a good-looking crack system near the left edge of the face that ran all the way up the wall. I hoped it would still be unclimbed when my cast came off.

As the sun neared the horizon, the light evolved into yellow tones tinged with orange. This was Sentinel's golden hour, and everyone stopped to gaze at it.

I joined the group of people gathered at the telescope, checking on the climbers. Yvon was above the roof now, diagonaling right over a blank-looking wall, trying to reach a crack that shot up the wall. It was slow going. He was probably placing some bolts. The sharp-edged sunlight made it just possible to tell who was leading.

TM was belaying in slings, dangling in an open book below the roofs. He was famous for his sense of humor. He had done the second ascent of the Totem Pole in Arizona with Bob Kamps, and its name was not an exaggeration: it was known as the thinnest pinnacle in the world. As they sat on its highly exposed summit, getting ready to rappel, TM suddenly shouted, "My God! I dropped the ropes!" Kamps gaped at him in horror—the ropes were gone! TM had tied them to one foot and dangled it off the edge, out of sight.

I bet he's not making jokes now, I thought. He's probably wondering if he'll have to spend the night right there. I knew he was looking down at us and envying our luxury, while we were looking up at them, on that golden wall, admiring their audacity.

Jan had returned from The Ahwahnee, and I assured her that TM would be OK—just one more night of suffering. Roper swung the scope back over to YPB, looking for the Teton climbers.

"*Still* not on the pedestal. They'll bivouac for sure!" He rubbed his

He opened with "Yarrow":[2]

> *There was a lady from the north,*
> *One scarce could find her marrow.*
> *She was courted by nine gentlemen*
> *And a poor plowboy from Yarrow.*

Mort sang on, and the tragedy unfolded, verse by verse:

> *As she walked down yon high, high hill,*
> *And down the halls of Yarrow,*
> *There she spied her lover done,*
> *Lying pale and wan on Yarrow.*
>
> *O Father dear, you've seven sons.*
> *You may wed them off tomorrow.*
> *But the fairest flower among them all*
> *Was the lad I loved on Yarrow.*

I noticed tears being wiped from many fair faces in the audience. Perhaps one of them would wander off into the dark with Mort afterward. As I left the campfire, he began his next song:

"Oh, I loved a lass and I loved her so well. . . ."

View from the Dihedral Wall, El Capitan

13
Dihedral Wall

Royal Robbins on the North America Wall, El Capitan

14
Nice Catch

"Congratulations. That was a textbook dynamic belay. A quicker stop would have zippered the whole thing."

I looked at my hands. The rope burns made my palms look like raw salmon fillets.

Royal looked at the collection of carabiners and pitons on his belay line, piled up against his swami belt. "I knew those pins would pop. I could feel each one pull out."

We sat there in our belay seats, munching gorp and drinking water. Then we braced our feet against the wall, leaned out, and scanned the wall above, looking for a route. It was hard to find one. Cracks wandered up, here and there, and ended in the middle of nowhere. Some of the rock looked loose and unhealthy—the color of overcooked liver. Huge black roofs seemed to block all progress.

It wasn't anything like the southwest face of El Cap, with its beautifully pure granite and long, seductive crack systems. That's why this other half of El Cap, the southeast face, had not been climbed. Now, in the fall of 1963, it was the greatest challenge in Yosemite. The era of fixed ropes was over,[5] but no one thought that the first ascent of a wall like this could be done by a party of two in one push. So this was a reconnaissance. We would go up for several days, search for a route, and rappel back down. Then we would spend all winter brooding about the possibilities.

"Get any good pictures?"

"Almost."

Royal looked back up the pitch.

"You mean I have to do all that again?" He was rearranging his rack of hardware, putting each tool in the right place. "That's real A5 up there. What a challenge. I'm not going to put in a bolt until I reach that blank spot."

I finished wrapping gauze around the palms of my hands and put the first-aid kit back in the daypack. I put the camera in, too.

"Ready?" he asked. His blood was up. He *had* to conquer that pitch.

"Just a minute." I pulled a bandanna out of my back pocket, tore it in half, and wrapped it on top of the gauze on each hand. It looked like there was going to be more heat.

Jim Baldwin on the Dihedral Wall, El Capitan

15
The Grove

There was a grove of ponderosas across the road from the Village Store. Grass and ferns covered the ground between them, and a brown, pine-needle-covered path wandered through. On the first day of snow the ground would turn white except under the trees, making a pattern of dark circles. On the second day they would be gone, and everything would be white.

After big climbs we had feasts there. We would get orange juice, just-roasted chickens, and a jug of wine at the store and walk over to the grove, sprawl out on the grass, and lean back against the tree trunks. Tart orange juice banished our thirst. We pulled the chickens apart with our bare hands, wolfed them down, and passed the jug around. Then I would lean back and watch the tops of the pines nod back and forth against the sky.

One morning Penny Carr and I were walking through the grove and met Roper coming the other way. He stopped and said, "Did you hear what happened to Baldwin?" He hesitated and then said, "You better sit down."

We sat down by one of the pines.

"He was killed last night—retreating off the Column."

Roper hesitated again, his eyes glancing back and forth between us, waiting for a reaction.

We stared at him.

"I just talked to Evans." He hurried through the story: Jim Baldwin and John Evans had started up the East Face of Washington Column. But the route was formidable, and late in the day, they decided to retreat. "You know it wouldn't be easy to rappel off that wall, with those overhangs and leaning corners."

I looked at Penny. She was perfectly still. Her mouth was open, and she kept staring at Roper.

"By the time it got dark, they were only a few rappels off the ground. They wanted to get off the wall and kept going. Baldwin went down the next rappel, with a hauling bag dangling from his waist, and had to swing over to a ledge. He reached for it, and missed . . . and came off the end of the rope."

Penny hadn't moved. She was still staring at him, and her face was very wet.

I looked down. An ant was wandering over the pine needles.

Roper cleared his throat. "See you back at camp." He got up and hurried down the path toward Camp 4.

Penny put her head in my lap and cried for a long time. I rubbed her back and watched the ant. It didn't seem to be getting anywhere. Then I looked up at the pines and listened to the sound they made in a breeze that didn't reach the ground.

I got up and walked around the grove, scuffing at pinecones on the ground, looking at the distant Valley walls between the tree trunks, thinking about the days and nights Jim and I had spent together on the Dihedral Wall.

I remembered a hot afternoon when I was belaying in slings and Ed Cooper was leading the next pitch. Jim prusiked up to me with a heavy hauling bag dangling from his waist. There were no ledges on that part of the wall, but we were hoping there would be one a pitch or two higher. Jim got out a seat sling and waited for us to finish the pitch, but it was slow going. Ed was out of sight above an overhang. We could hear him tapping on a drill.

Jim sat there, dangling on the rope just below me. He told me about growing up in a small town on a fjord in British Columbia. Before the Dihedral his biggest climb had been a cliff on another fjord—the Squamish Chief, near Vancouver. Long ago, after the ice age glaciers melted, the floor of Yosemite Valley had been a lake. It looked like a fjord, too, but it was far from the sea.

As we talked, shadows crept up the wall, the sun went down, and we watched tiny car headlights on the road far below. In the morning Jim was still in the same place, his head resting against the wall—asleep.

Later on, when we reached Thanksgiving Ledge, it was so spacious that you could walk around without being tied in. Jim took off his shoes and freed his tortured toes. He wiggled them and laughed. On that day he was a happy man. That's the way I remember him.

Warren Harding

16

The Rostrum

Two white spots on the river.

I wish they wouldn't do that.

I looked down at Harding. He had taken out the belay anchors, moved up, and was working on the next piton. The hauling bag continued its pendulum, almost touching the wall, then swinging out into space. In the middle of its arc, it crossed the line of the river, far below. That's where they were jumping in and making those white spots. That splashing was driving me crazy. I closed my eyes.

Ting . . . ting . . . ting.

His turn to work now.

Ting . . . tang . . .

That's better.

Tang . . . tong . . . tung.

The piton notes modulated down the scale as it loosened under the hammer blows. There was a hollow scrape and then a clank as he pulled it out of the crack and clipped it onto his hardware sling.

I opened my eyes. Warren looked up at me, and I nodded yes. He stepped up in his aid slings as I pulled in the belay rope until it was snug on his waist. He grimaced as he stretched up, reaching for the next piton. Then he settled back down and started working on the next pin.

The worst thing is the scum in my mouth. Yesterday I still had some slime to work with. Now the scum is caked hard, and I can't move it.

No. The worst thing is this weakness. On each pitch I run out of steam earlier and have to rest more. I was pretty shaky at the end of this one.

No. Here comes the sun. That's the worst thing.

I shifted my position, facing away from it. When the sunlight hit me, it felt like I was standing too close to a furnace and someone had just opened the door and shoveled in more coal.

Christ, it's worse than yesterday. It's killing us. I thought we'd be up before the sun hit again. The day is half gone already. I don't want to do that roof in the dark.

The North Face of the Rostrum. A nice little wall. It'll only take a day and a half, I had said. Looks like some free-climbing on the lower part. Aid on the upper half, but the crack system is excellent. It'll go fast. Overhanging the last few hundred feet, and no ledges. Some nice airy dangling up there, I said. Take a look with the glasses. See that roof on the last pitch? What a finish!

But what about this heat wave? Everybody came down from Half Dome and Sentinel. They were wiped out on the first day.

We'll only need one gallon of water, I had said. Drink nearly all of it the first day, so we'll feel good on the second morning. Then just a few hours of doing without. Zip right up those good-looking cracks and over the roof before the heat gets to us.

Why aren't there any clouds? This heat should generate some heavy storm action in the high country, big enough to drift down here.

It's never been this bad. It's worse than that time on the Leaning Tower, when we got to the sloping ledge after dark, out of water and croaking with thirst. George Whitmore went down to the car to get us something to drink. He came back up the talus and shouted up, but we couldn't understand what he was saying. So he walked out away from the wall and yelled some more, and we croaked back a little, but it made the thirst worse. So we gave up on getting any relief that night, and sat back on the sloping ledge to get some rest, with our feet in slings to keep from sliding off.

Then George started making strange sounds. Long noises kept coming up the wall, like he had appendicitis or something. He was mooing. We hadn't been able to understand his words, so he thought we might understand his sound effects. But we couldn't understand what a man mooing in the talus in the moonlight could possibly mean.

He had thought milk would be soothing for parched throats. And next day, when he brought it up, hot from the sun, we told him it was disgusting and nearly threw up.

So that night we had sat there on the wall, with George mooing down below. Warren told me about descending Mount Williamson in a blizzard, wallowing down through deep winter snow—it sounded lovely—barely

Warren handed up a sling. I took it, pushed the hauling bag aside, and clipped it into the main anchor piton next to mine. With a clatter of hardware he lurched up, clipped in his seat sling, and slumped down beside me.

He looked like a desiccated coyote. But a wolfgleam still glinted at the back of his eye.

I handed him the water bottle, sloshing it so he could hear how much water was left. He raised it and held it to his lips for a long time. I watched anxiously, but his throat didn't move. He lowered it, licked his lips, and almost managed a smile. The water sloshed as he handed it back—he hadn't drunk any.

I raised the bottle and felt the heavenly moisture on my closed lips, held it there awhile, then lowered it.

I handed it back. He raised it again, then so did I. I offered it back again, but he shook his head no. I sloshed the bottle again and put it back in the bag. The sound still hadn't changed.

Warren put his head against the wall and closed his eyes for a long time. His breathing was shallow and rapid.

The canyon floor rippled with heat waves. The ant people kept jumping into the river. The insect cars kept crawling along the road in slow motion. The sun was merciless.

Warren squinted up at the next pitch. It would end under the roof. He pawed through the hardware. Watch out for that angle with the broken ring. Belay rope runs here, there, then there. The loop of slack is clear, dangling away from the wall. Don't forget the hauling line. On belay, I nodded, and he started up the next pitch.

It's the third day and we're barely moving. That sun is killing us. My brain is frying. It's going sunnyside up. Come on, Thor, give us a blast. Better to be fried by lightning than baked into buffalo chips.

Attention all campers. A flash flood has struck the high country. It will hit the Valley in one minute. Dangling from cliffs is recommended. Look at them up there, Martha. Not much higher than they were yesterday. Yes, but don't you think they're doing very well, for buffalo chips? Did you check your knots today? Stop that damn splashing! When the Valley was full of ice, would we be off the ground yet? Let's go to Peru. The peaks are all snow. Listen to music from ice flutes and cornices.

There hadn't been any hammering for a long time. Warren's head was resting against the wall, his arms dangling. His eyes were open, but they were staring down at nothing. I got the bottle out of the bag and waved it. His eyes picked up the motion. He nodded yes.

I caught the hauling line in the air behind me, tied on the bottle, and he hauled it up. He held it to his mouth for a long time. Then the bottle came back down, and the hammering began again. I shook the bottle and listened to the water. He still hadn't taken any.

I raised the bottle in a silent toast to the man who would not drink the water he needed so desperately. All right, I won't either. When we reach the top, we'll finish it off together. That will be our victory.

When you wake up, the water jugs will be waiting outside your tent. They are made of green, blue, and clear glass and have a satisfying weight as you carry them over to the table. You look through the glass and wonder which color will make the water taste best.

When you mowed Grandma's lawn, the sun was very hot. The sweat built into a glaze, and when you then went into the house it was cool and dark. The big glass on the table was full of lemonade. You could hear the ice cubes clink as you lifted it. The sides of the glass were frosted with condensation. Large drops ran down, leaving a clear path where you could see the lemonade inside.

He's almost at the roof now. Better get ready to go. You'll be stronger after this rest. No you won't. Every rest comes sooner and takes longer. Each move you make is weaker than the last.

Yes, but you will always make one more.

A slow day in Camp 4

17
Dog Days

Upper part of Staircase Falls. Photograph by Keith Walklet.

18
Staircase Falls

I was at the ranger station signing out for tomorrow's climb when a teenage boy came rushing in with bad news. He and his friend had been hiking up the Ledge Trail, which ascends the south side of the Valley from Camp Curry to Glacier Point. Halfway up, they found a trickle of water emerging from talus at the top of Staircase Falls. It ran down a smooth slab and over the brink. They were thirsty and scrambled across to the stream, but his friend slipped on some gravel and went over the edge. The boy called down, but there was no response.

It was late in the evening, and there was no time to lose. I rushed back to Camp 4, rounded up some friends, and with a couple of rangers, we drove to Camp Curry.

Staircase Falls is thirteen hundred feet high and drops down the cliff in a series of steps, separated by diagonal ledges. Now, in mid-October, the falls were almost dry. We assumed the boy was dead but couldn't be sure. Perhaps he was alive but unconscious or was injured in a way that prevented him from calling out. He could be on any one of the ledges, or he might have fallen all the way to the ground.

We split into two groups. One group searched the base of the cliff, while the other charged up the trail, hoping to reach the top of the falls and start the search before dark. When we got there, we radioed the men on the ground. They had found nothing, so we knew he had to be on one of the ledges below.

It was dark by the time we made the first rappel. There were four of us. Unsure of the problems we would encounter, we had brought a large number of ropes and a full selection of hardware. We also had headlamps, a radio, and a body bag.

When we reached the first ledge, we carefully searched downstream and upstream, because he might have landed anywhere. We looked into fissures and under boulders and over the edge—he could be on a small ledge just below. We used hand lines whenever the ledge got too steep and smooth. It was slow, painstaking work—we didn't want to do it all over again if we missed him. It would have been much easier in daylight. He wasn't on that ledge, so we rapelled and searched the next one, and the next. . . .

The hours passed as we made one rappel after another. Eventually, we got to the last ledge. It was longer than the others and ended above the final big drop to the ground. He hadn't been found on the ground, so he had to be on this ledge. The others were ahead of me at this point. I could see their lights far down the ledge, flashing about here and there and finding nothing. It looked like our mission might be a failure.

I pulled down the rappel ropes, coiled them, and looked around. No hiding places here, but there was a pool of stagnant water nearby, the last remains of the falls for this year. I scrambled over to it and looked into its murky water. The bottom of the pool was a jumble of dark, mossy rocks, pieces of broken logs, and long tendrils of water plants. The beam of my headlamp caught on a thin line of white that seemed out of place. I reached in and swirled the water, washing the debris away. It was a tennis shoe. I tried to pick it up, but there was a heavy weight holding it down. It was attached to a human body. When it had hit the pool, it must have stirred up a cloud of mud and dead vegetation that had settled back down, covering the body and leaving only a small part of the shoe visible.

I called down to the others. They came back up, and we hauled the dead boy out of the water. The top of his head was missing. It was empty inside. I didn't want to see his face. His limbs were sticking out at strange angles and had to be straightened before he could fit into the body bag.

We carried him down the ledge to the drop-off. The first rappel ended in the middle of a blank wall, so we placed bolts for a relay in slings. I was lowered with the body bag, holding it away from the wall so it wouldn't scrape on the rock and wear through.

We reached the ground at dawn.

Southwest Face of Half Dome. Photograph by Ralph Anderson.

19

Planet Half Dome

The Mist Trail was jammed, and it was a drag plodding along behind all those people. Two endless columns of human ants clogged the granite steps, one going up, the other going down. Above Nevada Fall the horse trail came in from the right, and fresh, fragrant manure and clouds of buzzing flies were added to the wilderness experience. Tribes of Boy Scouts and YMCAers babbled and clanked along, stopping frequently to pick up the canteens and frying pans that kept falling from their overstuffed backpacks.

I left the trail and scrambled up to the crest of a ridge that descended from Liberty Cap. The rush-hour trail traffic was left behind. From now on, my only companion would be my shadow.

After descending the other side of the ridge, I entered a deep, cool forest. It was a peaceful stroll among the big tree trunks on a carpet of pine needles. A half mile farther I came to Lost Lake, a shallow pond a few hundred yards long. Half of its surface was clear water; the rest of it was covered with lush, green water plants.

I sat down on a flat rock shelf at the edge of the lake and leaned back against a log. Already, the crowded, dusty trail seemed many miles away. There was no sign of human presence.

I could hear a breeze high in the pines and occasional creaking sounds as two tree trunks rubbed against each other. The breeze didn't reach the ground, and reflections in the lake were clear and sharp.

Near the shore a few old pines had fallen into the lake. Their trunks were partly submerged, and their bare branches rose twenty feet into the air, like the ribs of sunken ships. In a few places small new trees were growing on the trunks, rising above the old carcasses.

Some mallards were dunking for food. When their heads went under the water, their orange feet stuck up in the air. In the distance I could hear a woodpecker drumming on a tree trunk. Two deer were browsing at the far end of the lake. At first they stared at me nervously, ready to flee, but when I didn't move for several minutes, I ceased to be a potential danger. They forgot about me and resumed feeding. It aroused all my old instincts for deer stalking.

Half a mile beyond the lake I could see the south face of Half Dome. Unlike the other Valley walls, it had no continuous crack systems. It didn't look anything like a mountain. Its smooth, rounded shape rose high above the forest like the monument of some unknown religion. It looked more like something to contemplate than to climb.

I could have spent the rest of the day in this place, but I had to move on. I followed a faint game trail through a narrow band of woods between the water and the massive slabs of Mount Broderick. At the upper end of the lake I came to a fine stand of mature trees: pine, fir, and incense-cedar. I looked back at the lake and at Mount Clark, rising in the distance. It looked very alpine, with sharp ridges, sheer faces, and couloirs filled with snow.

Above the grove, the slope changed to loose gravel, thick brush, steep slabs, and broiling heat. The fun was over. I thrashed and grunted my way up, trying to find the best route. There wasn't one. I alternated between bushwhacking and dicey bits of unroped climbing. As I worked my way up, my mind was invaded by a catchy tune: "Birds do it, bees do it, even educated fleas do it. Let's do it. Let's fall in love." I couldn't get rid of it. Every time I came to a new problem, it came back: "Birds do it, bees do it, even educated fleas . . ." Why was my brain doing this to me?

Now I was traversing left, grasping the brush with my hands, swinging from branch to branch while my feet skittered on the slabs below. I was heading for a small watercourse, hoping its bed would be easier going. It was. Even better, there was a trickle of water in it. I filled my water bottle to the top—this might be my last chance. After going up the watercourse a ways, I could see a group of trees on the left. I pushed through the last patches of brush and entered a shady grove of fir trees. The battle was over, and it was a pleasant walk to the brink of a huge drop-off.

This was the Diving Board. I found a flat spot where I could lie down and poke my head over the edge. It was a thirty-five-hundred-foot drop straight down to Mirror Lake. To the right was the great northwest face of Half Dome. I gazed at the crack systems on it. Some had been climbed, others had not. It was a fascinating game, linking up the cracks into what might be a new route. A few yards away I found the spot where Ansel Adams had set up his camera for his famous shot of the monolith. Just beyond it I could see the point of rock with a few trees that made up the foreground in his photograph.

As a reward for the day's work, I made a cup of Wyler's Lemonade and then looked some more. It was late afternoon, and the Valley was filled with hazy blue shadows. I could hear the sounds from nearby cascades and waterfalls, but in the distance Yosemite Falls fell silently, in slow motion.

It was hard to believe that during the ice age, the Diving Board had been submerged by vast glaciers. Later, as the ice receded, rivers of ice came down the canyons on both sides of Half Dome, merged just below me, and flowed down the Valley, sculpting its cliffs into the shapes known to humans. When the ice melted away, Yosemite became a lake, formed by the terminal moraine that served as a dam between El Capitan and Cathedral Rocks. I wished I could have seen it then. From the moraine I could have paddled a canoe up the Valley, tethered it to a wall, climbed up, rappelled down, and paddled away, as if I were climbing in Venice.

Across Tenaya Canyon I watched an eagle gliding down the Valley. As he passed by, I thought of the big eagle's nest perched on a ledge high on the east face of Washington Column. I wondered if it was his.

To my left the Diving Board continued as an elegant knife-edge a hundred feet long, heading west. Its left side was a steep, clean slab. On the other side was the void. It was an irresistible hand-traverse. I laced up my shoes and started across. The knife-edge was beautifully sharp and solid. Occasionally I peeked over the edge. The face below was breathtakingly pure and sheer. It was called the Porcelain Wall, and it had not yet been climbed.

After the knife-edge the ridge became a rounded slope, with an open grove of big Jeffrey pines, a wonderful contrast to that miserable bush-whacking. As I strolled along in the evening light, the "educated fleas" got replaced by my favorite theme from a Schubert symphony.

I looked back and finally had a full view of the southwest face of Half Dome, my objective for tomorrow. Earlier, I had been too close to it, but now I could see the whole thing and the crack systems that made it climbable.

I had decided to go very light, with only a daypack. The climbing gear had taken up most of the space, so I had no sleeping bag. Other comforts had been left behind, too—no extra clothes, cooking pots, flashlight, or matches for a fire. I had been training myself to get by on less. It was surprising how little you actually needed.

Dinner consisted of a few slices of salami and a hard roll. As it got dark, I put on my sweater and windbreaker and curled up in my bivy sack. It was one layer of waterproof nylon. This would help prevent heat loss during the night, but I would wake up damp from condensation. I was at seventy-five hundred feet, so it would be cold.

I got up early because the shivering had kept me awake for hours. The sun would come up on the other side of Half Dome, so the only way to warm up was to get moving. I packed up and scrambled along the moat between the wall and the brush until I came to the start of the route.

As I sorted out my gear, I could see long golden sunbeams flowing down Tenaya Canyon. The new light crept down Glacier Point, revealing the huge, dark shadow of Half Dome projected onto it by the sun. I was somewhere in that shadow, wishing I wasn't. When I had looked at the southwest face of Half Dome from Glacier Point on a sunny afternoon, the thought of making the first solo ascent seemed like a fine idea. Now it didn't. I was cold and alone and wished I hadn't told people about my plans. A little appendicitis began to seem attractive.

I couldn't just slink back into Camp 4 without trying, so I roped up, put on the hardware, and started to climb. Fortunately, the first pitch was not difficult. It went up cracks, flakes, and slabs, and gave me a good warm-up. A hundred feet higher I found an excellent horizontal crack and hand-traversed around a corner into an open book. On the third pitch I climbed up, then tension-traversed to a crack on the right, and continued up to a ledge.

It was good climbing, and my self-belay system was working well. At each belay stance I would hammer in two pitons and anchor one end of my rope to them. The other end was tied to my waist. I put a prusik knot on the rope, close to the anchor, and attached it to my waist with a sling. As I climbed, I slid the knot up the rope. If I fell, the result would be similar to climbing with a partner—I would stop when the rope came tight on the first piton below me. The impact might be strong, and the rope that formed the prusik loop was only one-quarter inch in diameter, so I added a second loop as a backup.

A second rope dangled from my waist, also attached to the belay anchor. At the end of each pitch I rappelled down, put on the daypack, and either climbed or prusiked back up, removing the pitons.

Now I was at the section of the climb that had established its reputation. A single thin crack went up the wall for hundreds of feet, over a roof, and out of sight. It was going to be difficult direct-aid climbing. Ever since the first ascent of Half Dome in 1875, climbers had wanted to climb a route that was not merely a matter of drilling holes in the rock. Back then, the northwest and south faces were out of the question. Attention was focused on the southwest face, which was lower angle but dismayingly smooth. Many attempts had been made in the 1930s and 1940s, but none were successful until John Salathé and Anton "Ax" Nelson arrived on the scene in 1946. Salathé was a blacksmith and had made special pitons out of hard steel that could be driven into marginal, incipient cracks. The other climbers had been defeated because their traditional pitons, made of soft iron, would bend and crumple in cracks like that, giving no support or security.

Salathé and Nelson had made the climb without drilling any bolts. Later climbers had found it necessary to place a number of them. Climbers with better skills had removed some of them, but as far as I knew it had not been done without bolts since the first ascent.[1]

Looking up, I could see that the crack was very shallow. It was too wide for a horizontal piton but too narrow for an angle, so I nested two horizontals together and hammered them in. They only went in an inch and a half and were a little loose. I added the tip of a knifeblade to tighten them up and then tied off my concoction with a loop of half-inch webbing, close to the rock to reduce leverage. After clipping in my aid slings, I pulled up on them and gave a bounce. The pitons held. I slid the prusik knots up a few feet, clipped in the rope, and stepped up.

The pitoning continued like that, and after much careful work I reached a ledge just big enough to stand on. The crack here was poor so someone had placed a bolt for a belay anchor. But just below the ledge, the crack was better. I placed three adequate pitons in it, tied them together for my anchor, and rappelled down.

After cleaning the pitch, I moved up to the ledge and removed the unnecessary bolt, which was only a convenience and not a necessity. The crack above got worse, and I started using my "Arrow" pins. These were soft iron horizontals made by Cassin and Stubai. I had hacksawed the blades so that they were only one inch long. They had been very useful on the Lost Arrow Spire, another Salathé climb. I tapped them in until the eye of the piton nudged up against the rock, providing a little extra friction. My connection to the rock was minimal, but I felt confident in my delicate carpentry. I came to another bolt but didn't use it.

Now the roof was just above my head. I reached out left, around it, and placed a piton in a crack I couldn't see. It sounded good, so I moved up on it, looked up, and saw that the hardest technical challenges were over. I put in belay pitons and looked down at my craftsmanship. A long line of pitons ran down the smooth wall, their carabiners glinting in the sunlight. They ended at my daypack, suspended in a place that looked impossible to get to.

The next crack was much easier, and I enjoyed seeing my shadow again, moving along next to me in strangely elongated shapes. The climbing was serious but standard, and I loved solving the sequence of problems it was giving me.

The pitch ended at another unnecessary anchor bolt. From there I made a long tension-traverse down and to the right, past another bolt, into the next crack system. To avoid using the anchor bolt, I had to leave two pitons behind when I pulled down the rappel. These maneuvers took some time, and suddenly I noticed I had lost my shadow. Big clouds were beginning to sail over Half Dome, and it looked like a thunderstorm might be brewing up.

The new crack system was a layer of exfoliation flakes that formed an open book facing right. I started up it with a new sense of urgency because of the clouds, but it was hard to go fast. Liebacking up the flakes wasn't too hard, and neither was placing pitons with one hand while holding on with the other. But it took two hands to loosen the prusik knots, slide them up, and tighten them again for an adequate degree of safety. The easiest answer would have been to let out a long loop of slack so that I could reach the next ledge before the belay rope pulled tight on my waist, but in that case any fall would be too long, and I might not survive it. So I muddled along, trying this and that. Sometimes the simplest answer was to place a few more aid pitons.

After a couple hundred feet I came to a place I had been looking for—a wide crack under a big flake. I peered in and saw a piton deep inside. This spot was mentioned in the article on the first ascent, published in the *Sierra Club Bulletin*. I reached in with my hammer and gave the piton a tap. It moved easily, and I pulled it out with my fingers. It was an old, rusty angle, and I examined it closely. Stamped on the steel, near the ring, was a diamond shape with the letter P inside, standing for Peninsula Wrought Iron Works. It was a Salathé piton from the first ascent—a real treasure.

I hustled up the rest of the route to a pine tree at the end of the roped climbing and signed the register. I had chopped out all the bolts, and the climb had been returned to its original quality. I wanted to read the historic pages of the register, but there was no time. Malignant cumulus clouds were piling up over Half Dome, and I could hear thunder in the distance. It would be a thousand feet of unroped climbing to the summit. I needed to get there and descend the cables on the other side to the trail before the lightning arrived.

I crammed the hardware into the pack, coiled the ropes and put them across my shoulders, and started up as the rain began to fall. The friction slabs were steep at first, and I had to be careful. Then the angle got lower, but the weather got worse. The rain was heavy, the footing was slippery, and the wind made me teeter back and forth like a drunk. Worst of all, lightning had arrived. It flashed at the same moment the thunder crashed, and I knew it would be unsafe to go any higher.

After stowing the pack in a solution pocket, I scrambled fifty yards to one side to get away from the hardware, which might conduct electricity. I put on the bivy sack, laid the ropes on the slab, and squatted on them, touching them only with my feet. I knew I shouldn't do that to my ropes, but it might save my life. The less contact with the rock, the better. Lying down would be more dangerous, so I hunkered there, looking like a glacial erratic wrapped in wet nylon.

Through a breathing hole in the sack I looked out at a strange, lifeless world. Slabs curved away in every direction and vanished into the clouds. Streams of water came out of the mists above and disappeared into the mists below. Everything was washed by rain, but nothing was growing. There were no plants or animals. Half Dome seemed to be its own smooth, rounded planet, and I was the only bump on it—a human erratic that could be washed away, blown away, or burned to a cinder at any moment.

The storm kept me from moving, relaxing, or thinking. There was no way to make time pass. Any thoughts kept getting shattered by the thunder and lightning. My only remaining capacity was dumb brute persistence.

Eventually the fireworks stopped, but the heavy rain continued, and I decided to wait until it lessened. I sat down on the ropes to relieve my aching legs. My mind began to wander, and I contemplated becoming a glacial erratic. That would be better than a tombstone. It needed to be granite, of course. No other rock would do, not even marble. It would be a boulder but also a sculpture, with noble proportions. It should stand on a slab that gleamed with glacier polish.

Then I started thinking about location. There were excellent spots on the rim, overlooking the Valley. I also knew of many fine places in the high country. I began with the Sawtooth Ridge and worked my way south to the Minarets, then to the Evolution country. I was in the Palisades when I noticed it had stopped raining.

I re-collected my gear—and myself—and climbed up into the clouds. On the summit, smooth slabs curved down on all sides and disappeared into the mists. The landscape slipped away, and I was standing on top of Planet Half Dome.

Season's end in Camp 4

20
Season's End

I left Camp 4 and walked along, hands in pockets, enjoying the feeling of having no objective in mind. It was late fall, warm in the sun but cold in the shadows. Half of the leaves were on the trees and half were on the ground. They were yellow, russet, and brown and made crisp, rustling sounds as I followed the trail past Swan Slab. It was a pleasure to be wearing loose, floppy shoes. The feet could relax along with the mind.

I turned up the path that led to the base of Lower Yosemite Fall. In June the waterfall had been roaring, and clouds of spray drenched the bridge. Now it was quite dry, and the silence was startling.

Heading downstream, I came to the place where John Muir had built his cabin in 1869. Just beyond was the remnant of an apple orchard, planted in the early 1860s. The apples were still tasty. The deer and bears thought so, too. After the lower branches were plucked clean, the deer would stand up on their hind legs and stretch their necks to reach the higher ones.

It reminded me of the time Penny had made a special meal out of things that grew in the Valley. She gathered acorns from the oak trees, leached out the bitterness, ground them in one of the Indian grinding holes in Camp 4, and turned them into flatcakes. I taught her how to catch trout, and they became the main course. She picked wild onions, mushrooms, and miner's lettuce and other greens from the meadows for a salad. Apples from the orchard were baked into a pie in a small oven over a low campfire. She squeezed apples to make apple juice. Unexpectedly, it fermented, giving the meal a special tang.

Nearby was a mature stand of oak trees. The golden leaves stood out against the black tree trunks. Squirrels were scurrying in the grass, looking for acorns.

A great wall, almost three thousand feet high, rose up behind the oak grove. Its main features were Yosemite Falls, the Lost Arrow, and Yosemite

Point Buttress. Much lower, four hundred feet above the ground, was Sunnyside Bench, a broad, vegetated ledge that ended at the brink of Lower Yosemite Fall. A popular 5.0 route went up its south face. It had been my first multipitch climb back in 1959.

Since then I had climbed it countless times because of the swimming holes at the brink of the fall. When the snowpack had melted, and the water volume was low, there were several fine pools surrounded by polished slabs.

I introduced a number of people to climbing on that route. I especially enjoyed taking women up it. When it was time to rope up, I said it was hard to tie a bowline backwards. So I would stand behind the woman and put my arms around her waist, tying the knot in front of her as I looked over her shoulder. I called this the Guide's Position. The rope would always be snugged up tight.

I soloed the route many times, climbing up and down it without a rope. The first time I soloed it, as a beginner, my boot got stuck in a jam crack. I could barely reach down and untie my shoelace without falling over backwards. After I pulled my foot out I climbed down and dislodged the boot with my hands. I tied it to my belt and finished the climb in one boot.

In later years, I started doing variations, right and left of the route, crossing over it in several places. Eventually I made a whole new route, much more difficult than the original. My self-assigned challenge was to do this harder route without a rope. Occasionally I would get in a tight spot and take a long time to figure out the next move. A lizard might scamper past me, running up and down the vertical, holdless rock. He would pause, do pushups, and look at me as if he were saying, "What's the matter, bud? You're not very good at this, are you?"

Sometimes in the summer the rock was almost too hot to touch, but when it was covered with snow in the winter, your fingers couldn't feel a thing. One time Sacherer had to place an aid piton on iced-up rock that we always did unroped.

I climbed it when my broken foot was in a cast. I guess that was the first one-footed ascent. I especially liked climbing it when the moon was full and gave everything a mysterious glow. It was strange to see my shadow at night, climbing up next to me in the moonlight. The air would be cool, but the rock would still be warm from the heat of the day. One night a girlfriend and I climbed it nude. I guess that was the first erect ascent.

Far above Sunnyside Bench was the Lost Arrow, a finger of rock two hundred feet high, attached to the great wall just below the Valley rim. It is usually climbed by rappelling down from the rim into its notch. The route then traverses to the outside of the spire and climbs to the summit over breathtaking exposure.

John Salathé was the first to attempt it. His partner failed to show up, so he tried it alone. He got halfway up, to a small shelf that became known as Salathé Ledge, before turning back.

Everything he did on that day was unprecedented. He was the first to make the scary rappels into the notch. The climbing was the first difficult, sustained direct aid ever done in North America. No Yosemite climber had endured such tremendous exposure. And he was doing it alone—unthinkable at that time. I've always thought it was the biggest step forward ever taken in Valley climbing.

One pitch above Salathé Ledge was my favorite belay spot in Yosemite. It was a tiny ledge almost big enough for two feet. I would anchor in, facing out, and gaze down at the meadows on the Valley floor, three thousand feet beneath my toes. The first time I was there, as a beginner, I didn't want to look at that shocking void. But later, with experience, I loved being there. I felt like a gargoyle perched high on the spire of a Gothic cathedral, looking out over everything. I felt like an eagle, though I had no wings.

At the ranger station I checked the sign-out sheet. It was early November, and most of the climbers had left Camp 4. But the weather prediction was good, and I was hoping for one more adventure.

I walked on to the Yosemite Museum. Inside there were big papier-mâché relief models of the park. Along one wall was a three-dimensional map of all the peaks and basins of the Sierra Nevada, from Yosemite to Mount Whitney, with dotted lines representing the trails and blue spots for the lakes.

There were displays of stuffed animals and birds. A mummified bighorn ram was positioned in front of a mural-sized photograph of Mount Lyell and its glacier. Park rangers had found its intact body in 1933, melting out of the ice at the bottom of the glacier. The ram had probably fallen into the bergschrund at the top of the glacier and flowed down in the ice for hundreds of years. I liked to think he had made the first ascent of Lyell before slipping on his descent.

A collection of butterflies was displayed on the balcony. They had amusing names, including my favorite, *Cercyonis silvestris*, the sylvan satyr. The label said, "It seeks to lure the pursuer ever deeper into the undergrowth."

Next to the museum was the employees' recreation hall, where table shuffleboard was one of the attractions. It wasn't used much anymore, now that the dorms had television. A new feature was Meredith Ellis's harpsichord. Meredith was a climber and PhD student in musicology at Stanford. She usually worked as a waitress in Tuolumne Meadows, but this summer her job was in the Valley, and you could hear her practicing in the rec hall every day between meal shifts.

Sometimes I would go in and listen while she worked on Bach. She would play a piece over and over until it was just right. Then she would pause and say, "And now, would you like a little Scarlatti?"

The next building was Best's Studio. With its shingled sides and stone chimney, it looked more like a house than a business. I stepped up onto the old, worn boards of the porch, where firewood was stacked high against the wall, in preparation for winter. Near the door was a giant photo of the Lost Arrow, taken by Ansel Adams. It showed John Salathé standing on the summit, and Ax Nelson rappelling off, after their first ascent of the Arrow Chimney.

Inside, a fire was glowing in the big fireplace. I warmed my hands and listened to the classical music that was playing. The room was filled with displays of American Indian art from the Southwest: pottery, silver and turquoise jewelry, and paintings. There were shelves of interesting books, recent best sellers and old classics, the finest selection in the Valley. The walls were covered with mural-sized prints of Ansel's most eloquent landscapes.

Ernie Johanson presided over this scene from the sales counter at the back of the room. Everything was arranged just so: The music selections were carefully chosen, the amount of heat from the fire was modulated, and a whiff of incense hung in the air.

The gallery with Ansel's photos was on the right. These were original 8-by-10-inch contact prints that showed his mastery of vision and technique. Afterward, when I went outside, I saw everything with heightened acuity, near and far, big and small.

I stopped at the post office and asked if I had any mail. Leroy Rust was behind the counter.

"Yes, sir," he said. "You sure do." Rusty was very energetic and enthusiastic. He pulled a letter out of the General Delivery box. "Is this the one you've been waiting for?" he asked with a grin. He gave it a sniff, raised his eyebrows, and rolled his eyes.

After handing it to me, he glanced around and lowered his voice. "You ought to marry that girl, you know. She's something special."

"Yes, she is, but I'm not ready for that."

"You guys," he said. "You people in Camp 4. You should all get married. Then you wouldn't have to do such crazy things."

The post office was a busy place. On the way out I met Father Murphy, the Valley's Catholic priest. He was interested in climbing and had invited me over to his house to talk about books on mountaineering. He was a kind and sincere man. He offered me some wine intended for use in church services. Since I wasn't Catholic, I thought it would be improper for me to drink it.

"Do not worry," he said. "It has not been consecrated."

Out on the steps I ran into Nic Fiore, who always had a beaming smile. He ran the Curry Company's ski operation at Badger Pass. During the summer he managed the hotel at Glacier Point and presided over the Firefall. Glacier Point was three thousand feet directly above Camp Curry. Every evening, a heap of fir tree bark would be burned down to a pile of embers. At dark it was slowly pushed off the edge, making a glowing red column a thousand feet high, before landing on a rock terrace and disappearing from view.

I walked on past Degnan's, a restaurant and grocery store. It and Best's were the only independent small businesses remaining in the park. Long ago, there had been many, but the Park Service wanted to simplify things and deal with only one concessionaire. It had pressured the two biggest, the Yosemite Park Company and the Curry Company, to merge and become the Yosemite Park and Curry Company—the YPC Co. Somehow Best's and Degnan's escaped.

The next building was the big new Village Store, a supermarket with a coffee shop and restaurant attached. When I first got to Yosemite, in the fall of 1958, the main grocery store was in the Old Village, which used to be across the river and close to the chapel. It had a creaky wooden floor covered with sawdust. Next to it was a café named the Greasy Spoon. On the other side was a movie house. Since the nineteenth century, the Old Village had been the social and business center of Yosemite, but it was all gone now. The area had turned back into a meadow.

I went into the coffee shop, sat down at the counter, and a friendly waitress came up. I had taken her up Sunnyside Bench. I ordered a hamburger and a lemon Coke. After a few minutes, she came back with a T-bone steak, baked potato with sour cream, and a big, thick milkshake.

"No. You shouldn't," I protested. "They might . . ."

"Hush," she said. "You look like you need it."

After I finished, she said, "How about some pumpkin pie with whipped cream? It's almost Thanksgiving."

I continued up the Valley past the garage where we all knew you should not take your car if it needed repairs. It took too much time and money to get it back. Instead, you should take it to Clyde Deal in El Portal. He was a climber and would treat you right.

The next repair shop was Lewis Memorial Hospital. Many of the Camp 4 denizens had spent some time there, under the cheery smile and talented hands of Dr. Avery Sturm.

Farther on, I came to the Church Bowl, where religious services were held outdoors when the weather was good. Church Bowl Chimney was just behind it. That was where my first climbing partner, Rob, and I had learned to chimney, a long time ago.

I crossed the road to the Ahwahnee Meadow, sat down, and leaned back against a favorite log. Penny and I often came here to talk, read, and make out. I opened her letter, and it reminded me of many things.

I recalled the time I carried her up the Yosemite Falls Trail on my back. I had just been invited to join an expedition to Peru, where we would climb twenty-thousand-foot peaks. We would have to carry big loads, and this seemed like a good way to get in shape.

There was deep snow on the trail, and more of it was coming down. I was used to zooming up that trail at high speed, but this time it took hours. I plodded up the switchbacks like a Clydesdale. The snow piled up on her hair, but it melted when it touched her face. She put her head on my shoulder and whispered Greek myths in my ear and hummed folk songs as I waded up through the snow.

After putting the letter back in my pocket, I looked up at the Royal Arches. By now, I had climbed that route many times, but I couldn't help smiling when I thought of that first time with Rob and Desert Frank. That was my worst time on the Arches, but now it seemed like the best.

The Ahwahnee was at the base of the Arches. I had worked there during the winter, when Robert Maynard was its manager. He had been the manager of Yosemite Lodge when I first arrived in the Valley. In the spring of 1959 he promoted me from busboy to bellhop, and this was a breakthrough. Instead of a split shift, I could work a straight eight. I always took the late shift, which began at 3:00 p.m., so I could climb every day.

Mr. Maynard was the manager when President Kennedy and his wife stayed at The Ahwahnee in the summer of 1962. Lookouts and marksmen were stationed on Sunset Ledge, directly above the hotel.

I walked over to the river and headed back down the Valley. At LeConte Memorial Lodge I saw the latest Sierra Club publications and looked fondly at the complete, leather-bound set of the *Sierra Club Bulletin*. I had spent many hours with those volumes, poring over their pages, learning the history of climbing in Yosemite and the Sierra Nevada, all the way back to the beginning.

I picked a volume off the shelf and turned to one of my favorite pages, where Bolton Brown described his first ascent of Arrow Peak in 1895:

> Of course, I wanted to climb it, but my feet were almost literally on
> the ground, rations were low and the future unknown. It worried me

a good deal, but just before falling asleep I decided that it would be foolish to attempt it, and that I would not. In the night I awoke and saw its snowy slopes gleaming serenely in the moonlight. At daybreak it was still there—it called me at breakfast, its rocky pinnacles beckoned me, its soaring summit challenged me. I could stand it no longer and hurriedly swallowing the last of my coffee, I threw prudence to the winds . . .

It seemed like he was talking directly to me.

On the mantel above the fireplace were relics of Walter Starr Jr.: his rope, ice ax, crampons, and knapsack. Above them, on the wall, was a photograph of the Minarets with Lake Ediza in the foreground. It was the last photo Starr had taken before falling to his death while attempting to solo a new route on Michael Minaret, in 1933.

I walked on down the river, skipping flat stones across it. Sentinel Rock rose up like a great hand, its flat palm facing the Valley, challenging climbers' eyes to find ways up it. At Swinging Bridge I gazed down at the upside-down reflections. A few trout were hovering in the current, their noses pointed upstream. Banks of golden poplar and cottonwood leaves lined the shores.

A lodgepole pine was growing on the riverbank. Its seed must have washed down from the high country. Up at Budd Lake it would be frosty by now. Ice would be creeping out from the shores. In the creek, splashes on the rocks would be turning to ice, and you would have to look sharp as you hopped across.

I looked up at the Valley walls that surrounded me on all sides. At first they had seemed impossible and unknowable. Now they were filled with memories of the great days I had spent up there with my friends.

The light was getting mellow as the sun neared the horizon, and the air had become very crisp. I wanted to have one last venture, but the first winter storm could arrive at any time. It would begin with rain, but then it would turn to snow. Sheets of ice would plaster the walls. When the sun came out, the ice would loosen and fall, spinning and glittering in the sunlight, slicing back into the wall and shattering into a thousand pieces. You wouldn't want to be up there then.

I walked across the tawny meadow, hands in pockets. Camp 4 was nearly deserted. Patterns of sunlight and shadow flowed over the ground and the empty tables. The tourists were long gone, and at last it was quiet. Even the denizens had departed. Now they were down in the flatlands, getting jobs or going back to school. But I knew they would come back in the spring.

El Capitan, with The Nose in profile

21
The Nose

S o there's the pendulum point above Sickle Ledge. The pitch after that ends at Dolt Hole."

"Right. And the next pitch is the pendulum into Stoveleg Crack."

"Man, that's a big one."

"It sure is. Looks wild."

Steve Roper and I were glassing The Nose of El Capitan. My car was parked on the shoulder of the road in El Cap Meadow. Our elbows were propped on top of the car, and we were looking through binoculars. Layton Kor was a ways down the road, throwing rocks at trees.

Stoveleg Crack shot straight up the wall for hundreds of feet, with no belay ledges. It ended at Dolt Tower, twelve hundred feet above the ground.

"Let's try to get to Dolt in one day," I said.

"What? I don't know, man. That's a long way."

"We'll start at first light."

"What if we don't make it? A bivy in slings would be a horrible way to start a wall like that."

"That's true. As soon as we get to Stoveleg, we'll see what time it is. If it's too late, we can retreat to Sickle."

"Across those pendulums?"

"They'll be easier from above."

"We'd have to lower the baggage, then haul it back up the next day, a big waste of time and energy."

Down the road I could hear rocks striking tree trunks. Layton had found a hollow dead tree, and the rocks made a satisfying thunk as they hit it.

"Kor!" Steve shouted imperiously. "Come here!" He grinned as he said it. They had a funny relationship.

Layton scowled in reply and then threw three more rocks in quick succession, with extra force—thunk, thunk, thunk—and came crunching over on the gravel of the shoulder. He was six foot four, strongly built, and seemed to be all angles, with huge hands and feet that stuck out of sleeves and pants that always looked too short.

"Glen wants to go for Dolt Tower in one day. What do you think?"

"I thought you guys knew about this route."

"That's right, we do. But what do you think?"

Layton grabbed Steve's binoculars, panned impatiently up the wall, and said, "Let's go for it."

Roper took a drink of water and cleared his throat. "Well . . . OK. If that's what you guys want. But I think you're asking for trouble."

The Nose had not been climbed for three years. Steve and I had watched the second ascent in 1960. They had taken two full days to reach Dolt Tower. We could have eased the problem by fixing a few pitches the day before, perhaps going all the way to Sickle Ledge. But now, in 1963, the rule was "no damn nibbling." It would have been called a fixed-rope ascent, not a continuous one.

The second ascent had taken seven days. We had learned a lot from watching it and thought we could make the third ascent in five. If we reached Dolt Tower in one day, we might even do it in four.

I scrunched my feet deeper in the gravel and panned the glasses farther up the wall, past El Cap Tower, then Texas Flake, and came to the notorious Boot Flake—a tall, thin flake barely attached to the wall. You had to nail the expanding crack that ran up its right side. Harding had zippered it on the first ascent. On the second ascent, Robbins had placed a bolt halfway up because it was so scary. One of Royal's forms of competition was to chop bolts placed by other people if he could do the climb without using them. Steve liked to compete with Royal and saw his chance. "I'm going to lead that pitch and chop Royal's bolt," he said, licking his lips in anticipation.

I put the glasses down, rolled my head from side to side, and rubbed my aching neck. Then I panned up even higher.

"Ahhh, look at that!" Roper said, as if he were looking at a beautiful woman. It was the Great Roof, a big, curvaceous overhang. Above that, a single, pure open book a thousand feet high shot up to the summit overhangs. It seemed to lean out over us. Were we going to climb all that in one go?

This was a different order of magnitude. The Nose pushed out into the forest on the Valley floor like the prow of some impossible ship. It surged up, huge and implacable, as if the master builder had used his best materials and carefully polished his creation, then made the other Yosemite walls out of lesser stuff.

Back in Camp 4 our preparations continued. Pitons were laid out on a table in rows, from small to large. First came the rurps and knifeblades. Then the horizontals: short-thin, short-thick, long-thin, long-thick. Next, the angles: regular, 1 inch, 1½ inch. Then the bong-bongs: 2 inch, 2½ inch, 3 inch, and a couple of 4-inchers.

"What about Leepers?" These were special angles with a Z-shaped cross-section, invented by Ed Leeper.

"They don't hold up to a lot of pounding."

"But that extra edge gives them more holding power. Good for expanding flakes, where you need to tap lightly."

"OK. Let's take a few."

The real workhorses of our collection were the horizontals, massive Bugaboos created by Chouinard. Made of chrome-moly steel, they could survive any amount of hammering. The second ascent had carried a hundred pitons; we thought we could get by with seventy-five.

Most of the climbing would be direct aid, so there was going to be a lot of pounding. Ordinary wooden-handled hammers would fall apart under such punishment, so we had special big-wall hammers. These were all-steel carpenters' claw hammers, with long handles so that each blow would deliver more power. One of the claws was hacksawed off, so you could use the other one for levering uncooperative pitons out of the cracks.

All the pitons were examined closely for minute cracks that might lead to failure. Then we inspected the ropes, foot by foot, looking for nicks and frays. We had to have complete confidence in our gear when we were in wild places on the wall.

We took four 150-foot ropes. Two were standard $7/16$-inch diameter. The leader would climb with one, and the man hauling the baggage would come up on the other one. The leader would trail a ¼-inch rope to haul up extra pins when needed. The hauler would have another ¼-inch rope so that he could let himself out from the anchor on diagonal pitches.

Roper made a new set of aid slings out of one-inch nylon webbing, because his old ones were getting frazzled. He made them long, with four steps, so he could get low to remove a piton or stand high in the top loop before moving off onto free-climbing. He clipped them to a tree limb, stepped in, and bounced up and down, cinching the knots tight. Then he lit a candle and melted the cut ends, so they wouldn't unravel. He made three slings. You only needed two for climbing; the other would stay in the hauling bag, ready for use in case one got dropped.

Our food was standard fare: salami, cheese, and hard rolls; gorp and chocolate bars; cans of tuna and sardines; Life Savers for thirst; and, as a special treat—a few cans of mandarin oranges. Our water ration was a quart and a half per man per day. We carried it in one-gallon Clorox plastic bottles that had been thoroughly washed out. They had metal caps that would not crack, the way the plastic ones did. After screwing them on tight, we wrapped adhesive tape around them for extra security. A hauling bag with water dripping from its bottom would be a disaster.

For bivouacs we had down jackets and single-layer nylon bivy sacks. A new item for me was an improvised cagoule, a hooded pullover jacket made for duck hunters. It was made of light, rubberized material, had no zipper or buttons, and was absolutely waterproof. It went down to the feet, but I cut it to midthigh length so I could climb in it.

There had been a lot of rain that spring and the weather prediction was not good, but we had to go for it. Memorial Day was less than a week away, and the summer ban was still in effect. No climbing was allowed on El Capitan from Memorial Day to Labor Day because of the traffic jams it caused at El Cap meadow. All attempts had to be approved, personally, by the chief ranger, Elmer Fladmark. Our interview with him had been successful. He agreed that we were qualified, but he would not grant us an extension despite the weather. We didn't want to wait until September because we might get drafted and never come back. Roper and I felt good about our chances. We knew a lot about the route, and if things got really bad up there, we had a secret weapon—we could unleash the hunting hound called Kor.

Friends gathered around the table and watched our preparations, offering advice and good wishes. Some of them looked a little doubtful, as if they might not be seeing us again.

We carefully stowed everything into two duffel bags made of strong, heavy canvas. The water bottles were at the bottom, wrapped in our down jackets to protect them from heavy jolts. The bags weighed fifty pounds each. In those days, before modern methods were invented, a heavy load was lifted by dangling it from your waist as you prusiked up the rope. Hauling by hand was no good because it would wear out your hands and arms and make them too weak for strenuous climbing. Thighs could lift more weight than biceps.

Prusiking was slow and laborious, and a fifty-pound bag made it worse. But Kor had brought with him an important new invention: Jumars, the first ones in the Valley. Made in Switzerland, they were metal handles that clamped onto the rope with a spring-loaded cam device. They slid easily up the rope but clamped tight when body weight was applied. With them, you could climb up a rope ten times faster than with prusik knots. They would make the hauler's job much easier. Kor and Roper had used them in the spring and swore by them, but I decided not to. The metal seemed light and flimsy, like cast aluminum, and might break if it was banged on the rock.

We had two daypacks, one for the climbing team and one for the hauler, who would be separated from them much of the time. These packs contained food, water, and extra clothes, enough to last the whole day. The hauling bags would not be opened until we reached the next bivouac ledge. Searching down through layers of gear during the day would waste a lot of time, and there probably wouldn't be a ledge big enough to put loose items on.

Everyone gathered around for a bon voyage dinner. Penny and her friends created a real feast. Then we threw ropes over tree limbs and hauled the bags and packs up into the air, safe from bears. Kor wrote a postcard to a friend in Colorado. The first line said, "Tomorrow is the big day!"

After dinner, after dark, we went off to our separate tents, to sleep. Maybe. I stared up at nothing—and everything. Lists of gear and supplies kept running through my head. I had to stop doing that. Penny's warmth was reassuring, but it couldn't solve my problem.

Many people had done short climbs at the base of El Cap, going up a few hundred feet to get a taste of it. Above that, the wall got steeper and smoother. It might be a thousand feet before the next ledge. Then it got even steeper, kept going on, and started to overhang. When you looked up at all of it, sometimes a little voice would whisper inside, "I can't do that. It's too big."

✦ ✦ ✦

The alarm went off at 3:00 a.m. I walked over to Roper's tent and said, "It's time." His voice came back instantly: "I know, man. I *know*." He woke up Kor, and we gathered at the table, where Penny was cooking breakfast in the glow of a kerosene lamp. It was probably the best one ever cooked in Camp 4, but we just chewed, swallowed, and stared into the darkness.

We lowered the hauling bags and put them into my car, along with the ropes and hardware. I kissed Penny good-bye, and we promised to meet on the summit.

There were no other lights on in the campground. All our well-wishers were asleep, like reasonable people. I let off the brake, pressed the clutch, and coasted downhill. At the flats I turned the key, put it in gear, and the engine came to life. I turned right, down the road, and watched the dashes of white paint disappearing into the left headlight. Everything else was inky black except for the sky, which was filled with stars.

The road went around a curve and suddenly Roper said, "Holy shit. Look at that." The left half of the sky still glittered with stars, but the right half was missing, blocked out by the mass of El Cap. The profile of The Nose separated the stars from the blackness.

I turned right onto a small unsigned road and, after half a mile, parked. Kor and I put the hauling bags over our shoulders, and Roper put on the racks of hardware and the ropes. Using flashlights, we followed a short, faint trail to the base of The Nose. It began with two hundred feet of class 3 scrambling. We rassled the bags up, pushing and yanking them from man to man, until we reached the ledge at the start of the first pitch. It was still dark. The air was cool, but our exertions had raised a sweat. We arranged the gear, put on swami belts, tied in, and waited.

From the forest below, I heard birds starting to sing as the sky to the east began to lighten. The summit of El Cap started glowing with the new day. Roper stepped left, looked up, and selected a piton. As he hammered it in, I could see sparks fly in the dawn light.

"OK, man. Here we go." He clipped in the rope and his aid slings and stepped up. The first pitch had good cracks. He placed each piton with a few blows and only bothered to clip into every other one. The first hundred feet went quickly.

"Watch me, man. I'm going off free. Let the slack run easy."

"OK. You've got it."

On the second pitch I climbed up, pendulumed right, and continued up on aid to a small belay ledge. Kor Jumared up with the hauling bags as Roper led the next pitch. This one was harder.

"It's A3 now," he said. "Watch me. This one's only in an inch. I'm moving up on it." It held, and so did the next ones. "I'm going off free now. Let it run. . . ."

On the fourth pitch, I climbed up and tension-traversed to the right. After placing two marginal pitons, I tension-traversed farther right from them, liebacked up a flake, and pulled up onto Sickle Ledge, the first bivouac ledge on the climb.

The next pitch was the only easy one on the route. I climbed it unbelayed as Steve helped Layton transport the bags across the ledge. At this point they switched roles. Originally, Steve had been scheduled to haul the entire day, but getting two fifty-pound bags all the way up to Dolt Tower, covering each pitch three times, would have been exhausting.

The climbing was going to be beautiful. The hard job was the hauling, so we were going to trade off on it each day. So far, our system was working very well. At the end of each pitch the leader would yell down, "On belay. The hauling line is fixed." The follower would climb up from piton to piton, reaching down to hammer them out, while the hauler came up with the first bag. After anchoring it at the new belay stance, he would rappel down for the second bag. He needed to get it up to the stance before the next pitch was completed, so that no time would be wasted on logistics. Thus, the two climbers worked only half the time, as they swung leads up the wall, but the hauler worked all the time.

The sun reached me, and I looked up. Dolt Tower looked impossibly far away, and I began to wonder if we could reach it by dark. The wall that rose above it looked endless and overpowering. I decided to not look at it anymore. I would just think about the next rope length. That was the kind of scale I could cope with.

Kor took the next lead. He climbed up to the end of the crack and pendulumed right, into an open book. I led the next pitch up to Dolt Hole, and this was where the fun began.

Layton nailed a left-facing open book, then clipped up a bolt ladder to its end—and now the show was on. I lowered him forty feet. The right wall of the book stuck out about three feet. He grabbed the edge and looked over it. Stoveleg Crack was a long way to the right, across a sheer wall, so it would be a running pendulum. Suspended on the rope, Layton walked left as far as he could, turned and ran right, leaped over the corner, and disappeared. In a second he reappeared, running left, then turned and ran right and disappeared again. He came back into sight more slowly and stopped.

"It's too far," he said. "Lower me down ten feet."

I did so, and he tried it again. It still wasn't enough. I lowered him five more feet, and he said, "That should do it."

"Go for it," Steve said urgently, as Layton started his swing again. When he reappeared, he was running all out to the left, making as high an arc as possible. Roper shouted, "Go, man, go!" Kor leaped over the corner, out of sight but came back again. As he turned, Roper yelled, "Go! Go! Go!"

This time he didn't come back. The pendulum rope started moving up, and we heard hammering.

"He did it!" Roper exulted. "We've got it made." Faint calls came down from above, the ropes pulled up tight, and it was our turn. After some complicated rope maneuvers, we joined Layton in Stoveleg Crack. My watch said 2:00 p.m., and we decided to go for it. But first we needed some food, so we sat there, dangling in slings, munching gorp, and watched the swifts zooming around and diving into cracks in the wall, to their nests.

The second ascent party had suffered terribly from intense heat. So, to deflect some of it, we were wearing white shirts, white pants, and white sailor hats to keep our brains from getting fried. We even had white hauling bags to keep the cheese and chocolate from melting and the water cool. Down in the El Cap parking lot, friends were watching our progress. Later, they told us we looked like a team of house painters up there. Of course, after all our preparations, the temperatures were cool, and heat was not a problem.

We were in an astonishing place—a perfectly sheer wall of white granite with a single crack that seemed to go on forever. No ledges in sight. This was the pure essence of El Cap. I had trained for years to get here, and now the dream was coming true. But it could only happen with a lot of hard work. I pawed through the hardware, shouldered a heavy sling of bongs, and started up Stoveleg Crack.

We moved up the wall like a three-piece inchworm. The leader would extend the creature, then the hauler would shorten it so that it could extend again. The belayer, in the middle, kept the creature organized so it could function efficiently. He should not have to say, "wait a minute" when the leader needed more pitons, because the extra hardware was trapped under the hauling bag, which was pinned down by the weight of the hauler, who was coming up the rope with the second bag and would need someplace to put it, too.

Layton and I swung leads through the rest of the day, and just before dark I pulled up onto Dolt Tower. Cheers came up from our friends in the parking lot. The ledge was covered with rubble, but comfortable pockets had been hollowed out by the previous climbers. For once there was plenty of room, so we just threw our stuff down in a heap. It had been a fine day's work, and we would sort everything out in the morning.

After a day like that it would have been nice to sleep in, but we had to keep moving. When I woke up, Kor was already rattling through the hardware, finding what he needed. Roper was peeing off the ledge, with a thoughtful look on his face. I would be the hauler today, so I could relax and watch them take off.

We were twelve hundred feet up. On some Yosemite Grade VIs, we'd be close to the summit by now, but on this one we were just getting started. Tactically, this would be our most challenging day because there were so many pendulums and traverses.

The first pitch began with a big tension-traverse into a tight chimney, then aid climbing led to a small ledge. The next pitch was mixed free and aid up a wide crack.

It was a pleasure to watch their teamwork. Each man could see what the next problem was and knew what the answer would be. But they had different styles. Kor was famous for his raw energy. He would climb jam cracks with a barely controlled fury, wedging and twisting his hands and feet as if he wanted to force the crack wider and turn it into a chimney. Steve was calm and smooth. He seemed to glide up the rock, transitioning from free to aid and back again with a graceful fluidity. When he took a piton off his rack it was always the right size, and he would place it with just a few blows.

Now they were enjoying themselves, and the banter flowed easily. "Come on, Kor. I saw you hold on to that pin. Pratt did it free." As Roper followed the pitch, Kor said, "What's taking so long? We'd go faster if we put you in a hauling bag."

Once the rope was fixed, I prusiked up with the first bag and rappelled down. After clipping the second bag to my waist, I put my weight on the $7/16$-inch rope and let myself out from Dolt on the doubled $1/4$-inch rope. When I reached the vertical, directly below the new belay stance, I pulled the $1/4$-inch through the anchor and coiled it right away, so it wouldn't get stuck in a crack below. When I reached the next ledge, Roper grabbed the end of my rope. Layton hauled it up and anchored it. Roper dashed up the pitch and quickly went out of sight on the next one. They were moving very fast, and it was going to be hard work to keep up with them.

When I got to El Cap Tower, Kor was perched on top of Texas Flake, a rope length above. El Cap Tower was the best ledge I'd ever seen. It could sleep ten people and was so flat you could play marbles on it. Halfway up The Nose, it was profoundly exposed and profoundly comfortable at the same time. I wanted to spend the rest of the day there, dangling my feet off the edge and watching the shadows change.

But the race was on. When I reached the top of Texas, Roper was already under way. This was the famous Boot Flake pitch. A ladder of bolts led out to the left on a perfectly blank vertical wall. The flake was out of sight, around the corner, and soon Roper was too. Layton and I sat there in suspense as the rope kept moving up. Then it started moving more slowly, and we could hear hammering. Now Steve was nailing the flake's expanding crack. Layton grabbed the rope firmly and controlled the amount of slack very carefully, ready to catch a fall at any moment. After what seemed a long time, Roper yelled down, "Off belay." Whew! Another challenge was conquered.

Now we began our most complicated maneuver. Layton started up the bolt ladder, trailing my hauling line, but I wouldn't be going to Boot Flake with them. The pitch after Boot was a long, wild double pendulum to the left, ending at a small ledge. When Layton got there, Steve would pull up their $1/4$-inch line and rappel down on it to the bottom of the Flake. Then he would tension-traverse on it to the pendulum point, as Kor pulled him over with the $7/16$-inch rope. After pulling the rappel rope down from Boot, Steve would repeat this process on the next pendulum and rejoin Layton. We had decided it would save time if I didn't have to repeat all this, with the baggage. Instead, I would bypass Boot Flake and traverse directly to the new belay stance beyond it.

As they grappled with the complexities of the pendulum pitch, I had a rare moment to relax. I looked down at the Merced River, winding through the Valley. It flowed west, into California's Central Valley. I had grown up in small towns on Highway 99, close to that river. As a child, I had played in white granite sand washed down from Yosemite. In summer, the sand was too hot to walk on with bare feet, but it was cool if you dug down. We lived on a road that was named El Capitan Way because on clear winter days you could see the great monolith, eighty miles away, capped with snow. I was nineteen when I drove to the Valley and saw them making the first ascent. Now, at age twenty-four, I was finally here.

The hauling line pulled tight, and I heard Roper yell, "The rope is fixed." It went across that bare, vertical wall, over vast exposure, and now it looked more like $1/4$-inch than $7/16$.

"What?" I yelled, pretending not to understand. I had to be sure. Roper gave me the same response. Of course, he would never make a mistake like that, but was it really OK to go out there?

"Whaaatt?" I yelled.

"The fucking rope is fixed!!" he screamed. "Come on!!"

That one sounded convincing.

Because of the double pendulum, the line would be very diagonal. This was made even worse by the fact that the Boot itself was well to my left. The diagonal was so severe that I had to let myself out using only a single strand of $1/4$-inch rope; the doubled rope would be too short to allow me to cross without letting go of it before I reached my objective. Then I would have no way to get back across for the second bag. After improvising a complicated brake bar that would provide enough friction, I traversed across and delivered the first bag to the new stance.

Back on top of Texas I set out with the second bag, this time on the doubled $1/4$-inch rope. I tied a loop in one end of it, clipped it to my swami belt, and let myself out. When I came to the end, I was suspended at the bottom of a V, held in place by one rope going up to the right and the other going up to the left. I took a deep breath and let go of the $1/4$-inch rope. One end of it whipped through the brake bar, and I took a big drop, down and left, toward the vertical. After I stopped swinging, I pulled the end of the $1/4$-inch rope through the Texas Flake anchor and moved up.

When I got to the new stance, I saw that Roper had led a short pitch and that they had left their doubled $1/4$-inch line on it for me. The next pitch was going to be another pendulum to the left, and they were climbing like demons. An afternoon thunderstorm had brewed up. It evolved quickly, and the clouds were developing menacing purple and black colors.

Layton finished the pitch, shouted down, and I took the first bag over. I had cut loose from the anchor and was coming up with the second bag when I was hit by an overpowering smash of blinding light and deafening sound that left me numb.

JEE-zuss!! Am I still here?

The pounding rain told me I was. After a few minutes I could move again. When I reached the ledge, Steve asked, "Are you all right? Christ, that was so close! I thought it melted the rope."

"It almost melted me," I said.

There was only one lightning bolt, but the rain continued. Streams of water were flowing down the walls, making rooster tails as they hit the ledges. Above us was the Great Roof. Curtains of water were pouring off its lip and being whipped away by the wind. We stood there in our cagoules and retreated into our solitudes.

After an hour, the rain stopped and the sun reappeared, as if nothing had happened. But forest fire smoke and the sound of chainsaws on the Valley floor told us that something big had come very close to us.

The sun started drying things off and steam began rising from the walls. We traversed a ledge to the left and climbed one more pitch to Camp 4, our objective for the day. It wasn't anything like Dolt or El Cap Towers, but was much better than nothing. Our bags and ropes hung off the ledge because it was so small. We sat there side by side in the last of the sunlight, with our feet dangling off into space, and felt intense satisfaction. The hardest, most complicated part of the route was behind us. Now the tension was gone, and we could enjoy being here. Roper had been impressed by some of Kor's leads, and now it was time to play.

"Layton Kor," he said, in deep stentorian tones. Then he changed to a higher voice: "Actually, it should be Latent Kor."

Layton looked at me and rolled his eyes. "I didn't think they let guys like him into national parks." Kor could play the game, too. "You know, when I got to the top of Boot Flake, he was blubbering: 'Layton, please save me! I can't stand it anymore. Get me off this thing.'"

"Oh, yeah?" Roper came back. "What's this?" He unclipped a bolt hanger with a mangled bolt stud in it. It was the one Robbins had put in on the second ascent. Steve had chopped it out on the lead because he was afraid Kor wouldn't do it. Layton was scheduled to do some major climbs with Royal in the summer, and didn't want to risk his displeasure.

They bantered on as I moved up to the next ledge and settled in for the night. The ledge they were on was big enough for one man. Mine was big enough for half a man, so it seemed about equal. At least it would be quieter up here. The last lines I heard from below were, "Stop picking out all the cashews" and "Don't piss on the ropes."

That Roper was a strange one, I thought. Exuberant and scornful at the same time. With less than a year of college, he had the vocabulary of a PhD. He relished using four-letter words, even in mixed company, but he also liked esoteric words, such as invidious and ubiquitous, omniscience and synesthesia, concupiscence and zoophilia. When he wasn't climbing, he was always reading, and for a long time there was a well-thumbed copy of *Look Homeward, Angel* on his table in Camp 4.

At first light I was looking straight up at the Great Roof. One pitch took us to the start of it. We stood on a small ledge and stared up, open-mouthed. The roof was awesome and beautiful at the same time. It arched out over us in a graceful curve, like the vault of a cathedral. A single crack led up to it. I nailed this until I reached the roof, which stuck out horizontally into space. Here the crack went right, in the joint where the vertical wall and the overhang met.

I selected a horizontal piton, reached out right, and stuck it up into the crack. It wedged in nicely, and I didn't have to hold it with my left hand to keep it from dropping out. One tap of the hammer secured it in place. It was a perfect crack, and after a few more blows, I clipped in. Even though it was an A1 pin, it always gives you a funny feeling to put your weight on one when it's driven straight up. I placed a row of pitons under the roof until I came to its end. A few free-climbing moves led right, to a tiny ledge and a bolt anchor. I reinforced it with a piton in the crack above, called down, and my partners began moving up.

The ledge was just big enough for my feet. Beneath my heels, the sheer wall dropped two thousand feet straight to the ground. Another thousand feet of it rose above me to the summit. It was smooth and vertical in every direction, and it seemed impossible that we could be here.

Roper cleaned the pitch and joined me on the ledge. Kor was a little white dot down below, letting himself out from the last belay stance. Steve looked up. "Incredible," he muttered. Once again, the weather had changed quickly, and the wall above was disappearing into the clouds. "Looks like it goes on forever."

As we climbed up into the mist and rain, the exposure disappeared, and we spent the day in a small world with no perspective. Sounds were muffled. Our vision was limited to a hundred feet in any direction. We knew where we were, but it was a matter of faith—there was no evidence. At one point the clouds opened, and we got a glimpse of the Valley. It was still there but farther away than ever.

The soggy conditions slowed us down. Late in the day we came to a difficult jam crack that the rain made even harder. It ended at the last bivy ledge on the route, Camp 6. It was a classic: flat, triangular, and big enough for three people. We climbed the next two pitches, left ropes on them, and rappelled back to our ledge.

The storm was clearing off, and, as the cloud fragments wandered among the Cathedral Rocks in the evening sunlight, I tried to capture the scene with my camera. It was getting nice out there, but we were buried deep in the open book, where the sun couldn't reach us. It was cold and damp. There was a steady tapping on my bivy sack from water dripping off the overhangs above.

Lying there, waiting for sleep to come, I thought about a night five years ago, when I left Mirror Lake at 2:00 a.m., flashlight in hand. As I went up the switchbacks, still under the influence of stories I'd read as a teenager, I couldn't help shining the light back down the trail, making sure a pair of yellow, hungry eyes wasn't following me.

I covered fifty-five miles of mountain trail that day. Now we were taking four days to go half a mile, and it was giving a deeper satisfaction.

✦ ✦ ✦

Our fourth morning was bright and clear, and we climbed up with gusto. We were still at full energy but showing some signs of wear. Our clothes and shoes were getting ragged. Elbows, knees, and toes were beginning to show here and there. Our hands were black from handling the hardware. Kor's fingers were cut and abraded from his battles with the rock. Roper's were smooth and unwounded because of his precise technique. Mine were in-between. They were a little stiff at first, but flexing them broke loose the scabs that had formed during the night, and they still served me well.

The open book was quite steep, overhanging in places, but the cracks were excellent, and we made rapid progress. By now the ground was so far away that we felt disconnected from it. We had become perfectly adapted to the vertical world, and it seemed like we no longer needed the comforts of terrestrial life. The granite architecture was magnificent. Our teamwork was seamless, and we could have gone on for days. Another thousand feet like this would have been a pleasure.

But it had to end. Layton led the summit overhangs. The hauling line came down in the air and curved in to our stance. I clipped on both hauling bags, and Roper lowered me out into space. He could have tied on an extra rope, but I said, "Don't bother—this will be fun." When he came to the end of the rope, he said, "Are you sure?" "Yes." With a mischievous gleam in his eye, he said, "All right, Denny. You're going to die!"

He let the end of the rope go, and I swung out into the void. It was superb and sickening at the same time. As I swung back and forth, I also started rotating because of twists in the rope. The weight of my body, plus the hauling bags, made the rope stretch. Each time I moved up, I could feel its diameter get thinner. Fortunately, it returned to normal when I was still.

✦ ✦ ✦

Friends were waiting for us on the summit. They had brought champagne and pastries, which were devoured in seconds. It was noon, and already the next storm was coming in, but it didn't matter now. We walked up easy slabs, signed the register, and took the trail back to the Valley as it began to rain. Roper, Kor, and the others charged ahead, lusting for the party that awaited us in Camp 4. Penny and I took our time. Four days felt like four weeks. The rain was cold, but it did not cool our heat.

Walking had a strange feel at first because I didn't have to hold on to anything. I seemed to be floating. Clouds covered the Valley rim, and it looked like Upper Yosemite Fall was pouring out of the sky. As we walked down the trail, I could feel myself transforming from a creature of the vertical world back into an earthly human.

That night, after the weather cleared, Penny and I slept in El Cap Meadow, close to the river. She said that while I was sleeping, I kept moving my arms and legs as if I were still climbing.

In the morning I watched new sunlight flow down the prow of El Capitan. It still looked untouched.

In memory of the denizens of Camp 4
who are no longer with us:

Jim Baldwin
Mike Borghoff
Penny Carr
Bill "Dolt" Feuerer
Warren Harding
Mort Hempel
Kay Johnson
Bob Kamps
Layton Kor
Rob McKnight
Chuck Pratt
Galen Rowell
Frank Sacherer

Notes

Prologue: Into the Valley

1. Years later I went back and saw that I was off-route and trying to do class 5 rock. In my eagerness to reach the crest, I had passed the inobvious class 4 continuation, which leaves the gully below the crest.
2. See glossary entry on classification of climbs.
3. At that time it was a two-lane, two-way road, with no wide shoulders to park on. When tourists stopped to look at the climbers, all traffic came to a halt.

Chapter 3, One Day on Whitney

1. Although it is now called Iceberg Lake, East Face Lake was the name used during the era covered in this book.

Chapter 7, Early Season

1. See glossary entry on classification of climbs.

Chapter 9, Bad Weather

1. Before brake bars and other rappelling devices became standard, climbers used a technique known as a Dülfersitz rappel. In order to obtain enough friction to control the speed of descent, the climber passed the rope through his or her legs, diagonally across the torso, over one shoulder, and down to the opposite hand. Climbers improvised various shoulder pads for protection, but the rope sometimes slipped off the pad and caused deep, painful rope burns on the neck or shoulder.

Chapter 10, The Icy Game

1. In those days, climbers filled out a form for each climb and signed back in when it was done, so the rangers could tell if anyone was overdue and perhaps needed rescue.

Chapter 12, Climber Central

1. The Yosemite Decimal System was not yet widely known. See glossary entry on classification of climbs.
2. This folk song is one of countless variations on the traditional Scottish border ballad "Braes o Yarrow," #214 in the Child Ballads. It was commonly performed and recorded under the shorter title of "Yarrow."

Chapter 14, Nice Catch

1. "Dynamic" here refers to the technique of dynamic belay; see glossary entries for "belay" and "zipper."
2. A4 refers to the difficulty of a direct aid pitch. See glossary entry on classification of climbs.
3. At this time, there was a heated controversy about the use—or overuse—of bolts. As Royal Robbins was a strong critic of bolting, he was particularly loath to place one here.
4. Of course, the belayer is supposed to keep both hands on the rope whenever the climber is moving, but occasionally the temptation to take a photograph becomes irresistible.
5. The previous big-wall routes on El Capitan involved the use of fixed ropes. Climbers would ascend partway up the route, then descend to rest and resupply, leaving ropes attached to the wall. This allowed them to regain their previous high point by ascending the ropes rather than reclimbing the route. However, as climbing skills and standards evolved, fixed-rope ascents gave way to continuous ascents, in which the entire route is climbed in one push.

Chapter 17, Dog Days

1. *Summit* was the first monthly climbing magazine published in the United States, running from 1955 to 1989, under the direction of Jene Crenshaw and Helen Kilness in Big Bear Lake, California.

Chapter 19, Planet Half Dome

1. It was considered poor form to add bolts to an existing climb, as it reduced the difficulty or danger from the standard established on the first ascent.

Glossary

aid climbing, direct aid: The technique of climbing by using artificial aids such as pitons, bolts, or other gadgets to support the climber's body weight when the rock lacks hand- and footholds.

aid slings: Loops of nylon webbing that a climber attaches to an anchor and uses as a ladder for stepping up.

anchor: A point of attachment established for the purpose of belaying, rappelling, or security on a climb. It can be set up with hardware such as pitons, bolts, or cams, or it can make use of natural features such as tree trunks, rock horns, or flakes.

approach: The hike to the start of a climb.

belay: To use a rope to protect a climber. The belayer, who is stationary and anchored, pays out the rope while his or her partner is climbing and remains alert to catch any falls. *Dynamic belay* is a technique used for a leader fall—the belayer lets the rope slide through his or her hands at first and then cinches up, bringing the leader to a gradual halt to reduce stress on equipment and the leader's body.

big wall climb: A long and difficult route that typically takes more than a day and requires climbers live on the route, hauling up gear and supplies.

bivouac, bivy: A night spent on a climb, with minimal shelter (called a bivy bag or sack) or none.

bolt: Expansion bolts placed in the rock using a drill and fitted with a hanger to allow rope attachment; used for protection, aid, or anchors in the absence of suitable cracks for pitons. Their use was controversial, as they permanently altered the rock, and their overuse could reduce the standard of difficulty.

bong-bong: An extra-large piton. Its name is derived from the sound it makes while being hammered into a crack.

bowline: A knot used by climbers for tying into the end of the belay rope. It is complicated to learn and easy for beginners to tie incorrectly.

brake bar: A device used in rappelling to add friction on the rope to control the speed of the descent; may be a commercial device or improvised from carabiners.

bucket hold: A big hold that is very easy for a climber to grasp and pull up on.

carabiner: A metal oval link with a gate on one side, like a safety pin, that climbers use to connect ("clip in") to the rope or to an anchor.

chimney: A crack wide enough to hold a climber's body; it is ascended by using cross-pressure from feet, hands, knees, or back braced against both walls (a technique called chimneying).

chopping bolts: Removing bolts that are considered to be unnecessary.

cirque: A bowl-shaped, steep-walled mountain basin.

classification of climbs: The difficulty of Yosemite climbs is described according to three aspects: grade, class, and direct aid (if applicable).

Grade refers to the length, scope, and overall seriousness of a climb. In Yosemite at the time of this book, grades ranged from I, for climbs taking only a few hours, to VI, big walls requiring days of commitment.

Class designates difficulty of climbing, ranging from trail walking (class 1) through unroped scrambling on rocks (class 3) to climbs that involve technical moves and require protection to avoid serious injury in case of a fall (class 5). Within class 5, difficulty is more precisely defined by using decimal points (e.g., 5.0, 5.2, 5.7), with higher numbers indicating more difficult moves; this is often called the Yosemite Decimal System. In class 5, also called free-climbing, the rope and hardware are used only to protect the climber in case of a fall, not to assist in ascending.

Direct aid means that the climber uses equipment to ascend and is ranked on a scale of A1 (easy) to A5 (extremely difficult).

cleaning the pitch: Removing the protection or direct aid placed by the leader, usually done by the following climber.

direct route: A largely straight, and usually more difficult, vertical route up a wall or peak.

expanding crack: A fissure in the rock that widens with pressure, as when gear is placed in it, rendering the protection insecure.

exposure: The void beneath your feet when you are far above the ground on a steep cliff.

face hold: Any feature on the surface of the rock that can be used as a hand-hold or foothold—ledges, edges, depressions, nubbins, etc.—in contrast to cracks or chimneys.

fixed rope: A rope left anchored to a wall, allowing the climbers to ascend by prusiking or Jumaring rather than climbing the rock itself.

flake: A slightly detached piece of rock, usually with a thin space behind it.

friction climbing: Climbing low-angle, smooth rock that has no holds or very small "microholds."

Jumar: A device for ascending a fixed rope; it consists of a metal handle with a spring-loaded cam that allows it to slide up easily but clamps the rope tightly when weight is applied.

knifeblade: A very thin piton hammered into incipient cracks.

leader: The person who climbs up the pitch first, placing and clipping into pitons or other equipment for protection. The leader is belayed from below and thus faces far greater danger than the follower. For example, if a fall occurs twenty feet above the last protection, the leader will fall forty feet. In contrast, the follower climbs up while the leader pulls in the rope from above, so any fall will be very short.

lieback: A strenuous climbing move in which a climber pulls out on an edge of rock with the hands, while using the feet for counter-pressure against the wall.

munge: Dirt and vegetation filling a crack.

nailing: Hammering pitons into a crack for direct aid.

off-width crack: A crack too wide to ascend by jamming in hands or feet but too small to fit the body inside for chimneying.

open book: A wide vertical V-shaped feature on a rock face; also called a dihedral.

pendulum: A climbing technique in which a climber is lowered on a rope and runs back and forth to gain enough momentum to cross an area of blank rock to reach another crack system.

pitch: A section of a climb that can be covered in one rope length.

piton: A metal spike that is hammered into cracks for protection or direct aid; comes in a wide range of sizes and configurations, including angles, knifeblades, and horizontals.

portaledge: A foldable platform, usually equipped with a rain fly, that can be suspended from anchors, allowing climbers to stretch out and sleep on a wall in the absence of natural ledges.

protection: Equipment such as pitons, bolts, or cams placed to reduce the climber's risk in case of a fall; not intended to be used for direct aid in ascending.

prusiking, prusik knots: A method of ascending a fixed rope by using a loop of nylon cord tied around the rope with a special knot (called a prusik knot), which slides up the rope easily when unweighted but cinches up tight when supporting the climber's weight. Made obsolete by Jumars.

rappel: To descend steep rock by sliding down a rope; the speed of the descent is controlled by wrapping the rope around the body or by using brake bars or other specialized devices.

roof: Rock that protrudes horizontally from the wall.

runner: A length of nylon webbing knotted or sewn into a loop. Also called a sling.

rurp: A piton the size of a postage stamp, designed to fit into tiny, shallow cracks.

scree slope: Steep, unstable piles of rock fragments at the base of a mountain or cliff.

solo climbing, soloing: Climbing alone. The climber may use a rope and gear to self-belay, or may climb without any protection at all.

stove-leg piton: Pitons made from the legs of an old-fashioned stove, used on the first ascent of The Nose of El Capitan.

swami belt: Webbing wrapped several times around the waist and secured with a knot; the belay rope is then tied to it. In case of a fall, the wide belt would put less strain on the body than a single loop of rope would.

tension-traverse: A climbing technique in which a climber leans against the rope while being lowered from a piece of protection, then uses hands and feet to move sideways across the wall.

tie-in: Where the rope is attached (tied into) to the climber's swami belt or harness.

webbing: Strong fabric woven as a flat strip or tube, usually knotted or sewn to create a loop (called a sling); used for many purposes in climbing, such as holding gear, climbing direct aid, or belaying.

zipper: A leader fall that pulls out a long series of pitons.

Index

About the Author

GLEN DENNY climbed the sheer walls of Yosemite Valley in the 1960s. He is renowned for his striking photographs of both the Golden Age of Yosemite climbing and life in historic Camp 4, which have been published throughout the world and collected in his book *Yosemite in the Sixties*.

Among his partners were climbing pioneers Warren Harding, Royal Robbins, and Layton Kor. His first ascents in the Valley include the West Face of the Leaning Tower, the Prow on Washington Column, and the Dihedral Wall of El Capitan. He lives with his family in San Francisco.

PHOTO: PEGGY DENNY

Through the support of donors, Yosemite Conservancy provides grants and support to Yosemite National Park to help preserve and protect Yosemite today and for future generations. Work funded by the Conservancy is visible throughout the park, in trail rehabilitation, wildlife protection and habitat restoration. The Conservancy is also dedicated to enhancing the visitor experience and providing a deeper connection to the park through outdoor programs, volunteering, wilderness services and its bookstores. Thanks to dedicated supporters, the Conservancy has provided more than $100 million in grants to Yosemite National Park.

yosemiteconservancy.org